Introduction

The National Institute of Neurological Disorders describes autism as:

A range of complex neurodevelopment disorders, characterized by social impairments, communication difficulties, and restricted, repetitive, and stereotyped patterns of behavior.

What this means for us is that my son cannot tie his shoes or brush his teeth. He did, however, just learn to dress himself (although he prefers to be nude). He has great difficulty using utensils to eat. He was toilet trained at twelve. He likes to head-butt to show affection, which can be quite painful to receive. He does not talk more than a few words. Has never told me he loves me.

According to Autism Speaks, there is a 1 in 88 chance your child will be autistic. Boys are four times more likely to be autistic than girls. Meaning that today if you have a male baby, there is a 1 in 54 chance the child will be autistic.

Each year more children are diagnosed with autism than juvenile diabetes, aids and cancer, combined. There is no known cure.

Heavy stuff.

My son JJ is autistic: I am his father and a standup comic. (A neurodevelopmental disorder and comedy, only this time it's not the comedian who is suffering from it [hey-oh]).

I talk about autism. I refuse to be shamed into silence.

I talk about it on stage. Most people enjoy it, but some people get uptight when, from the stage, I talk about how my life is touched by autism. A few think I should not discuss it; that I should ignore the proverbial elephant in the room that is my life. It is hard to ignore something that drives almost every decision you make; where you live, what kind of job you can take, how you spend your money, what your housing will be like, whether or not someone wipes their ketchup covered hands on your shirt as you leave the house.

Autism is not something to be embarrassed by; it is not pleasant, but it is part of my life. A part of life I did not choose but a part nonetheless.

People talk about being aware of autism; in fact, there is a month dedicated to "awareness". What does Autism Awareness mean to me?

That you/we should be aware. Aware of what you ask?

That people are different. We all have different skills, abilities, strengths and weaknesses.

That people are all equal, but not all the same.

And that is ok. Yes, JJ is in intensive therapy to improve. Yes, we moved across the country to get him the best care we could. Yes, he is getting better, but not at the pace we would like.

There are things that you or your kid could do at age three that my teenage son still cannot do, and may never be able to do. And that is ok. His life, even with his limited abilities, is not a tragedy.

He is who he is and the situation is what it is. In addition to being autistic he is a 14-year-old boy with all the normal angst that comes with his age.

To me the point of Autism Awareness is not that I expect every person I come in contact with to work for a "cure" for my son, but that they would be aware of him. Cut him (and us) some slack when we are out. He is not being autistic to make you angry. He did not get out of bed this morning trying to "be autistic" just to slow you down at the store.

Maybe we are not the worst parents in the world. Maybe we are just average people in an extraordinarily difficult circumstance doing the best we can. Maybe you would handle the situation better: maybe not. We may never know. (Although you could find out: Adopt an autistic kid and test your skills. Then I welcome your advice, comments, and insults, no matter how harsh.)

Rice Krispies with Ketchup:

A Comedian's Journey with an Autistic Child

Kirk Smith

Kirk Nathaniel Publishers

New York London San Salvador Bucharest Dallas Guayaquil

To me, "awareness" means that you would be "aware" that autism puts people in a difficult circumstance. Maybe that mom at the store with the kid her size having a melt down is doing the best she can. Maybe, instead of judging, you could offer to help her with her groceries? Or at the very least, give her the benefit of the doubt and don't pile on by saying hurtful things like some of the ones that have been said to me:

"What is wrong with you?"

"What is wrong with him?"

"Can't you control him?"

"What a brat."

Just be aware that the person you are dealing with has different challenges, that are probably difficult for you to even understand, but we would appreciate it if you could go the extra mile and extend them grace. This is what "awareness" means to me.

I try to remember that life, even an imperfect one, is precious and fleeting. Life has taught me a few things. If there was a way I could sit a younger me down and explain a few things (and spare myself some pain), through funny stories, this book is how I would do it. (The stories are true, but names have been changed to protect the innocent…and guilty.)

Life is a gift, even an autistic life. Life is a journey. The gift is always the journey, never the destination. [i]

This is mine.

Advice to a Younger Me

YOU'RE NEVER READY

There is no way around it. This book is a weird little collection of stories. It's about my strange little journey. As a kid, my family moved everywhere. My parents were going to change the world, which to me meant, "Kids...we are moving".

I am the son of a Pentecostal preacher man, going back four generations on one side and on the other side, grandpa was a coal miner. Before that, according to my aunt, we were bootleggers, and pretty good ones too.

We moved several times in the US before I was five, and then to the mysterious lands south of the border. The first place we moved was El Salvador during their Civil War in the early 80s. San Salvador was dangerous at the time. Often we would see dead bodies in the streets. Our house, like all of the others in the capital, had bars on the windows, doors, and surrounding the carport.

I had two little brothers and we would climb the bars, pressing our faces against them like monkeys trying to escape.

The war meant we did not get out much. The only people I saw consistently were the soldiers at the Taiwanese embassy in front of our house and the garbage men. I wanted to be a solider...Wait; no...I wanted to be a garbage man. Sure soldiers had guns, but they had to just sit there. Garbage men had it made. They rode around hanging on the back of trucks, yelling "Basura!" (garbage), and hurling bags of filth. What's not to like?

We went to a little local Spanish speaking school. No English. Well some people thought they spoke English, but they didn't. My brother had almost platinum blond hair and the kids loved to touch it. They had never seen anything like it. Oddly enough, my brother's first words in Spanish were, "No me toques" (Don't touch me).

Grade school was not fun. Everything was new--new language, new friends, even the games were new. And during the civil war, where people are dying in the streets, even the kids wanted to talk politics.

Third grade brought with it a new school. One of the first weeks there, three little boys, who towered over me, cornered me.

"Which party do you like?"

I knew this was a trick question but just didn't know the right answer.

The one party, Arena, was red, white and blue and the other party (PDC) was green. USA is red white and blue, so maybe that was the right choice. But wait, they don't like America this week, maybe I should say Green? But wait the word Gringo has the word green right in it. It is pronounced "GREEN-go."

"Green?" I say raising my eyebrows and shoulders in unison, and half smiling.

Punch to the stomach. Apparently, Green is the wrong answer.

Getting punched in the gut as a kid always felt like your world was ending. You would never again get air inside of you. The wind that had been forced out would be the last you ever breathed.

"No, you like Arena!" I was informed.

At that point, I just liked air. I was not familiar with either party's stances on the economy, unemployment, or the IMF; however I did know my stance on being punched in the stomach. I was not in favor.

"Arena," I mouthed silently and nodded from my position on the ground.

The next day a different group cornered me near the bathroom exit.

"Arena or Green?"

Oh boy. Ok, these are different guys, are they friends of the stomach punchers?

"Arena?" I say again raising my eyebrows and shoulders like an insecure marionette.

"No, you cockroach, you like Green," one said with a push.

I nodded fervently. "Green, right." The two political parties arguments had been reduced to me trying to not get punched or pushed.

I don't think anyone was happier than me when the elections were over. Kids can be mean but they are nothing compared to kids with a political ax to grind.

Today, I have kids of my own. They are teenagers now.

My youngest, as I mentioned earlier, is severely autistic along with some other issues, which, for better or worse, currently drives many of my decisions. We moved to New York City from Dallas several years ago so my son could go to a special school here.

My daughter is fine. Actually she's way better than fine. She is a gift, an incredible person. She was my first-born. She was born in 1997. She was beautiful and not just because she was my daughter.

Everyone always says their daughter is beautiful and then shows you a picture and it is all you can do to not blurt out, "Where is your daughter? Is she standing behind that little troll?" Not that kind of beautiful. She really was. She was healthy, sweet, and easy. When she was little she liked to dance, sing, play, and ate whatever we gave her. No colic and she potty trained herself at a year and a half. She was an easy baby if there ever was one.

In 1999 Michael Jordan and the Bulls won the championship, Lewinsky was still in the news and I found out my second born, my only son, was autistic. While none of the above came as good news, that last bit was definitely the worst of it.

We knew something was wrong at about a year and a half. JJ, our son, stopped talking almost all at once. The dozen or so words he knew were replaced with grunts and cries. He took to sitting in the corner for long periods of time and not answering to his name even if we were standing next to him. He would not even turn if we stood directly behind him and yelled his name.

Before this I was able to interact with him, play, sing; but now he would look at me for a second before quickly getting that far off look on his face. He would travel to a far away place in his mind, emotionless, or worse, with screams and howls.

We thought he might be deaf but with his language gone, we were not sure how to check. The answer was a complicated neurological test where they put him to sleep to check his hearing.

We took him to the hospital where they prepared him for the procedure. My wife tried to warn the staff that he was very spirited, strong and would not just sit there and let you put a needle in him. They assured us that they knew what they were doing and we were relegated to the waiting room.

A few minutes later he came running out of the room, in his little gown, free as a bird, little buns poking though the back of the gown.

He was sprinting, laughing and babbling incoherently. He was happy, smiling and bouncing off the wall as he sprinted down the hall. He was high.

A heavyset nurse burst through the doors a second later.

"Someone grab that little boy."

There was no way she was going to catch him. He had a head start and was carrying 200lbs less. Another nurse down the hall grabbed him.

My wife: I tried to warn you he is fast.

Portly Nurse: Fast and wily. He pulled out the IV and jumped off the bed in one motion. He is a live wire.

As the second nurse carried him back, he was starting to fade. He was trapped in one of his giggling fits that he tends to get caught in. Laughing so hard he cannot catch his breath. Winded by his own happiness. Through the years I have often witnessed his delirious giggling, where the funny overwhelms the present, and all he can do is laugh so hard that he forgets to breathe. These are my best memories of him. In this case, he was doped up, sure, but happy, laughing, and trying to escape the authorities. A rebel without his pants.

The tests confirmed our worst fears--his hearing was fine. All signs pointed to some other mental problem and his new habit of hitting his head against the wall seemed to align with that diagnosis.

Several doctors told us that he was fine. They explained that sometimes little boys are different and that he would out grow it, but we were sure there was something else going on. We continued to try to find a definite diagnosis as to what had happened to our baby.

Before his second birthday, a doctor sat us down and told us, "There is something wrong with your child. He is autistic." The word did not mean much to me until I looked up what it meant.

[ii]In the US this year 1 in 88 parents will hear this same news. It is the fastest growing developmental disability in the world. If you don't know someone with an autistic spectrum disorder, then you're just not looking hard enough.

At the time, I was underemployed, working at a factory. Working but unfulfilled and not making the kind of money you hoped to make when trying to provide for a family of four. Autism did not seem as pressing as putting food on the table. Surely not having a good job at the moment is the worst bit of news, right? Wrong. For better or worse, that diagnosis has informed most of my life decisions since then.

I had my kids in my early twenties. I was not ready. I thought I was ready, but I just was not.   I was especially not ready to be the dad of a severely mentally handicapped child. There are things that I know now that would have been really helpful to know then, it would have saved me a lot of pain. I did (and still do) have a really hard time with my son's condition.

I wish a wise old man, who had already gone down this path with an autistic child, had told me a few things about parenting. Now I am neither wise nor old, but I have been on this path for some time. Maybe you can glean some knowledge from my mistakes. If so, please do. This is my journey.

NOT NORMAL

We defined autism as a developmental disorder that affects the brain's normal development of social and communication skills but how does this manifest itself?

[iii]Some of the early signs of autism include lack of eye contact, losing words, repetitive behaviors, not hitting the typical milestones of a developing child intellectually or socially. Autism is not a form of brain retardation. The best analogy I have heard is, think of the brain as a computer. The brain itself is the hardware, the brain activity being the software. With autism there is something wrong with the software. All the hardware is there but the connections (synapses) are not firing correctly so the brain is not functioning as it was intended.

Most people know very little about autism. I remember when I first told my friend Mike, who doesn't get out much, about my son, "Yeah, my kid is autistic."

He said, "What is wrong with your kid being artistic, a lot of kids are artistic. Not everyone likes sports."

So I had to explain what autism was. I tried to explain that it was a developmental disorder surrounding communication and socialization, and mentioned some popular characters in films with his condition. Then he comes back with, "Oh, I think I get it." He pauses and I can see the wheels slowly turning in his mind, and then he comes out with, "we should take him to Vegas and get paid!" Then I have to explain to him that no, he is not like Rainman. He is not the kind of autistic that likes numbers; he likes ketchup and running around naked. When people think of autism, they think of savants like the character Dustin Hoffman portrayed. However, only 1 in 10 autistic people, are savants.

When my friends brag about their kids, I can't help but feel a little jealous. Honestly, I have a hard time with it. My instinct is to make jokes.

Them: "My kid's on the honor roll."

Me: "Well, my kid stopped peeing in the closet…except for at your house. Don't make me get that bumper sticker, 'my kid is peeing on your honor roll student.' It's really long."

In some ways, my son is just like everyone else.

He got a credit card in the mail. Not the application, the actual card. Which I guess makes sense. He is part of the last group of Americans without credit card debt, autistic children. I just want to be part of the marketing campaign. I imagine it going something like this:

Three cases of ketchup, $72.00.

One box set of the Wiggles, $29.00.

Being autistic and having a better credit score than your old man…priceless.

Other than credit card offers in the mail, our lives are far from normal. As unusual as my childhood was, I naïvely thought I would grow up to have a normal life.

I graduated from college after four quick years of basketball, like a west coast Forrest Gump. Entering college, I was sure I was going to the NBA. I was 6'2", skinny and white, what could possibly go wrong? It didn't work out.

When, shockingly, I was not drafted by a single one of the 30 NBA franchises, I decided to pursue the American Dream. I was sure I would lead a normal life, and in a way, I guess I am.

The Autism Speaks' new campaign states the odds of your kid becoming Tommy Hilfiger are 1 in 23 million. The odds of him being diagnosed with autism are 1 in 88.

Unfortunately, for many people, autism is part of the new normal. The fact that it is more common does not make it less stressful. It is important to find outlets for stress and anger. I don't recommend this for everyone, but I started boxing.

It helps me blow off stress. Plus, I needed to get in shape and be able to fight off my daughter's suitors.

I don't recommend trying to learn how to box in your late 30s. It is an unforgiving sport. It is one of the few activities where, if you make a mistake, the consequence is a man who is trained to punch, gets to punch you in the face.

Now when I started I was 209 pounds, which made me a heavy weight. There are a few problems with that. My joints are like that of a Japanese woman, and by that I mean small and frail, not polite and deferential.

If you could see me, you can tell, I am not built for Fight Club. I am built for Pillow Fight Club. Sure we still meet in basements but we mostly sit on pillows and make soap.

The weight classes in boxing are based on weight, not muscle or talent. The heavy weight division is 209 pounds to forever. So I was a heavy weight. You know who also is a heavy weight; Butterbean, King Kong, and Andre the Giant. You can be a good heavy weight at around 210 but I was a 180-pound man with a 30-pound belly, not the ideal heavy weight.

So, my first fight I am set up to fight a guy who is 6'5" 250 pounds of anger, broken childhood dreams, and tips from Grand theft auto. I was, how could I best describe my feelings: I was scared.

The day of the fight came and he did not show. My trainer said, "Maybe...he was scared of you", and we laughed and laughed.

No one is scared of me. Wild animals walk right up to me. Deer eat crumbs off my face. Babies take candy from me. Creampuffs want to eat me.

Soon it was time for my second fight. Now in boxing they teach you to block and dodge punches. I blocked 9 punches; but I did not block the other 49 punches. I don't know if you have ever been punched in the face 49 times. It stings a bit. Don't add it to your bucket list. You're not missing anything.

My trainer had a tip for me:

Trainer: Your problem is you look really tense in there. You need to relax.

Me: Well, I don't find it particularly relaxing to be punched in the face.

Trainer: Yes, but look at him. Look how relaxed he is.

Me: Yeah, 'cause no one is punching him. It's just me in there, crying. I think he finds my tears and crying relaxing. But ask him, I bet his hands are killing him. Or he's at least a little worn out from all the punching.

I've lost some weight since then. Now I am around 180 pounds, which means I am fighting people that are built more like me. You know, normal.

My third fight came. About an hour before I fought, I got into a huge argument with my wife. I went to the gym and beat this man like the proverbial redheaded stepchild. Afterwards my wife was asked, "How did it go?"

I said, "You owe that man an apology 'cause I opened a can of whoop a** (read bottom) on him. And I think he was confused because while I was hitting him I was yelling 'I don't care how much money your ex-boyfriend Steve is making or what he is doing.' And he was like, 'I don't even know a Steve? Who are we talking about?'"

I actually didn't really beat him up. It was close. I won. But I don't think he'll ever watch Blues Clues and ever see that Steve character the same.

I have always loved sports. I am not good at most of them, but I enjoy the activity, the energy, and the competition. And when I was in school, sports provided me with a place where I could belong. I was never going to be valedictorian, but a letterman jacket seemed achievable.

My daughter is 15 and is talking to me about wanting to go to Oxford. I was not thinking about Ivy League schools when I was her age. When I was 15, I was thinking about boobs and basketball. And to be honest, not much has changed. Basketball drove absolutely everything I did growing up. From my clothes, to my hair, to whom I hung out with and what I smelled like, my life was all driven by basketball.

It determined where I went to college. I ended up going to my parents' alma mater, Bethany College in Scotts Valley, California. I was not recruited to play basketball out of high school, and Bethany was one of the few places I figured I could play. The conversation with the coach went as follows:

Coach: Well, you can walk on.

Me: How does that work?

Coach: No guarantees. You try out, and we'll see how it goes.

That was the end of my recruitment. Universities were not falling over themselves for my athletic skills. That is how my NAIA basketball career started.

Everyone wants to play Division 1, but not everyone is built to play Division 1. Some of us are more suited to Division 8. But since there is no Division 8, I played NAIA. NAIA means playing mostly Division 2 and Division 3 schools. Unlike Division 2 and 3 schools, NAIA schools could give full ride scholarships. But it was a purgatory of sorts. You would have guys like me who could not make Division 1 and then you would have the Division 1 castoffs. Players who were athletic enough to play but had other issues. We had Berry Thompson who had set a record for three pointers at New Mexico State, but then had been accused of rape. Or Steve Johnson who just could not seem to make grades, or read. It was an eclectic assortment of drunks, and misfits with a few of us that were all heart and no athletic prowess. Think of the movie Rudy but without the happy ending and more hazing.

Our coach was an old warrior, John Block. He set the scoring record for USC, PAC-10 and the country. He went on to play 10 years in the NBA and was even an all star once. He was tough, old-school tough. He was the type of tough where, if the broken joint was not out of place you keep playing. If it was out of place, you put it back in place, and kept playing.

He was 50 years old, 6'10" about 250 pounds with a piercing stare and the scars from battling the NBA greats. And his fingers did not look right. Bending in the wrong places with knots where there should be no knots or not bending where they should bend. He thought they bent but they did not bend.

Once, during a timeout, he called us over. "I want you to run this," he said, and then held up his fingers. There were 10 digits all right but they were going this way and that. Some bent at the first knuckle, others, caring nothing for their brothers, pointed off into space. No one said anything. We had no idea which of his fingers he was "holding up", but no one had the heart to tell him. Finally, I said, "We can't tell which fingers you are holding up Coach, what number is that?"

"Gosh darn it! That's 53! Can't you see? That finger is down, that one is up, and you know I can't move my index fingers!"

It was rare if you got a "gosh darn it." His language was usually saltier. However, he did not need salty language to make you feel dumb. He could degrade you without dropping a single f-bomb. "Smith, do I have to get my seven year old niece out here to run these drills? Seriously, what is the problem? Were you dropped on your head? Do you need a personal invitation, princess?" One of his favorites was simply shaking his gigantic head in disbelief and scrunching up his face, "Boy, you are dumb".

He left the NBA right before the big money came into the game, something he was well aware of. He played against the great, Wilt Chamberlain and Kareem and his body showed it.

It was a different time in the 70s with illegal drugs and steroids.

On one of the long drives to a road game, I asked him once if he took steroids back in the day. "I don't know. We didn't know what steroids were back then, you took what ever pills the team doctor gave you."

Oh the seventies. When athletes followed doctors blindly, because the doctor knows best, even if the doctor dispensed advice through cigarette-clenched lips.

As tough as his practices were, they were nothing compared to trying to navigate life with an autistic dependent. Getting yelled at is not the same as the metaphorical punch to the gut that autism can deliver. The latter can change everything.

I think that is the biggest piece of advice I would give a younger me. If I could travel back in time using Doctor Who's TARDIS time machine, I would try to warn myself: You will not live a normal life.

You won't have a "regular" life. That is just how it is. There is nothing wrong with that, some things will be better, but it will not be normal, plain and simple.

Whether it is taking separate vacations.

Getting uninvited to church.

Or fighting to get your child the very basic care that they need.

Things are going to be different.

Different good, and different bad.

We will cover some bad later; let's cover some of the good.

After a few years you may find yourself much less interested in material things (especially after many of your favorite things have been damaged and destroyed).

And while that may be frustrating, you will start to appreciate other, more important things.

I appreciate my health.

You may really appreciate your relationship with your other child(ren). I deeply treasure my relationship with my daughter.

I try to teach her everything I would teach a boy or a girl. I talk to her about school and her interests but also interact with her at a different level. I explain to her how stocks work, what derivatives are, how to block a punch, how to throw a punch, how to set up jokes. In short I have a much deeper relationship with her than I might otherwise have had if my situation were different.

Your relationship with your spouse will be forced to develop. Statistics for the divorce rate of couples with a special needs child are not good. You love that person, but you will also need them as a full and complete partner. You will know them and they will know you like few people know each other. The discomforts of daily life will force you to ache for a connection, not to take away the pain, but to share the pain, reducing it by half. It's a wordless connection that is hard to create without the pressure and heat created by the difficulty of your situation.

Things have changed and you will not be living a normal life.

Enjoy it.

INVEST IN YOU

An Autistic kid; a Sisyphean Task.

I don't know what I am doing with my son. I don't understand why he is handicapped or how our lives will play out. I often feel like I am making no progress. Sometimes I feel like Sisyphus.

Sisyphus is the story of a king who rebels against the gods, cheats death, and is caught and punished. His punishment is to push a rock to the top of a hill, only to discover in the morning; it has returned to the bottom and needs to be pushed to the top of the hill again. This continues for eternity.

Sisyphus' story reminds me of another story. A story I heard of a father and a son. The father tells his son, "Push that rock." The son pushes the rock for years, it does not move.

After some time the son confronts the father. "You told me to push that rock, but it's impossible. I could not move it."

"I did not tell you to *move* the rock. I can move it. I told you to *push* it. Pushing the rock will help you develop your muscles. It gives you purpose. It gives you meaning. It makes you strong. The exercise was about you, not the rock."

The endeavor, no matter the outcome, has consequences. Pushing an unmovable rock (or a special human) produces results, if only on the pusher.

Yet Sisyphus' story was one of punishment. Or was it?

Homer believed that Sisyphus' struggle made him the wisest among all men, something he would not have been without struggle.

Is it really only a punishment, if we allow it to be a punishment?

The gods would cause the rock to be at the bottom of the hill in the morning, but it was Sisyphus' will that would power the push back to the

23

top. After years of waking to the rock being at the bottom of the hill, he would have known the push to be futile, yet he would soldier on.

Why?

When Sisyphus walks down the hill to start the process of again pushing the rock up the hill, what is his countenance?

Is it still a punishment if, as he walks down to the bottom of the hill, he laughs? Is he still a tragic figure if day after day he rises to the challenge?

Sure some days suck, but not every day. I wonder if some days he would laugh as he bent over to put his shoulder to the rock. If the first movement of the rock up the hill, made him smile; if sometimes he would get pumped as he approached the top. Yelling. Face red. Covered in sweat. Happy. Alive.

When the rock rolled down the hill, did it always infuriate him, or from time to time did he enjoy the view up top before walking down below? Did he saunter down the hill? A man. All muscle and sinew. Ripped. A man whose body obeyed him.

Has he not become strong? He has pushed a stone to the mountaintop for millennia. Has it not had some affect on him, as he has had on it? Has the stone not turned him to rock, powerful, full of strength and life, allowing him to cheat death another day?

Is he still to be pitied if, as he strolls to the bottom, he examines the road he has created pushing that rock up a hill and having it roll back to the same place?

Perhaps the point of pushing the rock up a hill is to develop my muscles.

Maybe the point is not the movement of the rock.

You may not move the rock, but the rock will move you.[iv]

I am biased, but I think exercise is important. I would tell my younger self as much. I would say, you count. Invest in you.

While you should not chase happiness, invest in yourself.

There are things that you want to do that bring you a measure of joy (that are not at someone else's expense). Do them.

They are different for everyone. For me it is standup comedy, boxing, traveling and riding motorcycles. For you they could be biking, skydiving, knitting, or painting. Do it. (Not all at once - that would be a mess).

You are older, your kid is mentally challenged. You are tired.

Yeah, it will be harder now. Do it.

You will have to carve out time. Do it.

You may not be able to do it at the same level or with as much intensity as before. Do it. (Starting to catch the theme?)

Whatever it is that you love to do, or have wanted to do, do it. Make the effort. It is important; now more than ever. You need to find areas of your life that bring you joy and pursue them.

You need to invest time in yourself and not derive all of your identity from the care of another person. You are still you and need to do the things that bring you fulfillment and joy.

It will be harder and more complicated, but it can be done.

You can do it.

While caring for someone else, it is easy to fall into the trap of not allowing yourself down time. And I don't mean down time to watch "The Real House Wives of Whatever", but to invest in you; to recharge your batteries. If you don't, you will burn out. A burnt out you will not serve society or your family better.

We learned this lesson the hard way (which I call the "Smith" way). As a family, we (and my wife especially) went through a very painful chapter leading to my wife having to be hospitalized. If I had to do it again, I would have paid or begged whomever I had to, to get some babysitting, help, or relief. We also would have started doing the separate vacations sooner to make sure she got a break. There are a thousand things I woulda', coulda', shoulda' done differently for my family. It was a very painful lesson. Again, we learned this one the "Smith" way.

Younger version of me, invest in you. If not for yourself, then for the others that depend on you. (Especially you moms, I am talking to you.)

Best quote from *The Matrix Reloaded*:

"But then if we do not ever take time, how can we ever have time?"

You matter. You count. Take time, to have time, to invest in you.

SAY THANK YOU

Mental illness is not something I like to dwell on. When I consider my son's condition and what that means for my future, it can wear me down. I try to consciously choose to be positive. That is something that took me a long time to figure out.

I think one of the keys to life is to try, try, and try to find the joy in your situation. There is joy in even the saddest corners of your life. Search for it. It is there.

There is a reason there was humor in concentration camps. In what was arguably the darkest chapter in human history, people needed to smile and to laugh. It was not because they were trying to pass the time, or that they wanted the attention that comes from telling a joke. It was because they needed a measure of joy. In the book *Man's Search for Meaning*, author Victor Frankl, a former concentration camp prisoner, speaks in depth about the search for humor and how it helped prisoners survive.

Humor will help you survive.

One of my favorite movies of the 90s was *Life is Beautiful*, which recounts the tale of a man and his family taken to a concentration camp by the Nazis, and his quest to keep the camp from breaking his son's spirit. It is a heavy story, but in the end it shows how humor has the power to lessen the sting of loss.

Search for joy. It is stupefying, perplexing, and elusive, but can be found. Search for it.

Autism is a sad deal. Sometimes it can make me sad to talk about it. I still have not seen *Temple Grandin*, the biopic of Temple Grandin, an autistic woman who overcame her limitations to become a PhD in animal science. I hear it is great. And I am sure it is. But the movie is too close to home. I have a hard time whenever I have to confront my son's condition, its limitations on him, and what that means for his future and mine. I will watch the movie someday; I am just not there yet.

I definitely don't have it all figured out, but I daily try to find the funny in what my life has become.

Trying to find the joy in autism is one of the things that led me to standup comedy. It allows me the freedom to try to see things a little differently. When I talk about autism at a show and we all laugh about it (not at my son, but at what it means and how it affects us), it allows us to laugh at a bully (autism) who has and is savagely beating me.

While I am still taking a beating from autism, a group of strangers getting together and laughing at said bully greatly alleviates the pain. It allows me to defang the autism dragon and see it for what it is. It is not an end-all, but just a nuisance who would try to take as much joy from me as it can. And it is, at least partially, up to me to determine how much I will allow it to take. I will take my beating (thank you sir, may I have another?), but it will not take my joy.

I will try to see the lighter side of life and not take myself (or my situation) too seriously. In some ways, getting "beat up" is just part of life.

I am not saying that everyone should become a stand up comic (I don't want the competition), but I am saying you need to search for ways to find joy in your life. I guarantee you it is there. Scour the earth. You will not be disappointed.

Look for the funny. Look, laugh, live, and love.

Now in my quest to find the funny, sometimes I take it a little too far. I have an irreverent sense of humor. Few things are off limits, especially when dealing with my friends, family, or wife.

My wife is used to my shenanigans by now. We met at the beginning of 1994. She had just moved from Sri Lanka to California to go to college. Sri Lanka—what a hilarious name. Go ahead, say it out loud, "Sri Lanka." It has a magical, almost fake sound to it. It sounds made up. I had to check a map to make sure it was real.

Turns out it was real, and she was real.

So, I am super white and my wife is brown. She's not black, just black-ish. Like black enough to get us kicked out of Connecticut, a Klan rally, or a Cracker Barrel.

When you have been married for more than 10 years, you (or at least, we) give each other nicknames. Ours are a little racist. My nickname for my wife is "Chocolate Buns", and her nickname for me is "White Backup Plan".

When cell ring tones came out, she gave me the music from Andy Griffith show because she said I looked like Opie from that show. You know the super white guy that is gullible and knows nothing about anything. "Gee shucks partner, tell me more about this 'hip-hop' and 'alcoholic elixirs' I keep hearing so much about."

In my lifetime, the country has gotten really touchy about the Middle East.

My wife is not from the Middle East, but the TSA agents think she is, so I thought it would be funny if when she calls me on my phone it plays the Muslim call to prayer. I was wrong; it was hilarious.

In keeping with the theme, I nicknamed her "the Taliban" because she is little and brown, and I know she is going to be the death of me.

The idea being, if I am hanging out with my friends and she calls, I say, "Sorry fellas, fun's over. It's the Taliban on the line, I got to go." Everyone has a good laugh. I had this ring tone for about a year.

Everything was fine and dandy until I was on a domestic flight. Domestic carriers like to fly planes designed and manufactured by the Wright Brothers, so, not surprisingly; there was a mechanical problem on the antique we were flying.

The year before, some idiot tried to stick explosives down his pants (and was successful only in burning his own nether regions). So now, every time I go to the airport, someone touches my junk.

Because there is a 1 in 10 million chance someone will bomb a plane, I have to submit myself to be touched 100% of the time I choose to get on one. I would rather take my chances that I am on that 1 plane in 10 million that will blow up, rather than know with certainty that someone will touch my privates every time I go to the airport (and have nightmares that night).

The TSA has inadvertently created the employer of choice for perverts. "Are you looking for a job where you can touch between 80 to 200 balls per day? Maybe run some fingers over strangers' bums? Does your current job look down on you groping customers? Then make a change. TSA is the only way. We touch more balls by 8 am than most people touch all day."

But I digress. I get to the plane. Before take off, we are on the tarmac with mechanical problems. There is no air-conditioning. We are all just sitting there. Everyone is pissed.

A phone starts to ring. It's mine; I forgot to turn it off. And it's my wife, so yeah, the Muslim call to prayer starts to emanate from my pocket.

The guy next to me looks like he could be Middle Eastern and turns nervously towards me.

And I'm trying to play it off and say, " No, it's my wife."

But I have changed her name in my phone to "the Taliban", and when I get my phone out of my pocket, he can see it says that "the Taliban" is calling me.

He is looking at me like I just got the "Bat Signal" (or the "Osama Signal", as the case may be), and I am supposed to do some crazy Taliban thing.

So he says, "Oh, are you Muslim?"

I say, "No!" and I accidently make a face of disdain. "No, it's my wife."

"Oh, is your wife Muslim?" And I say, "No," and accidently make the face again. I immediately felt like an idiot.

30

Then I have to explain to him that, "No, I am not a racist. It's just that the Taliban annoy people, and my wife annoys me, ergo, she is the Taliban."

Kidding aside, I like my wife. She is ok.

She likes me too…usually, though not always for the reasons I thought she would. That is something else I would tell my younger self.

When you get older, you find out your wife wants your body, just not the way you think. When you have a disabled kid, she needs you. No I'm not talking about sex, dates, or flowers. Nope, she needs you for the boring mundane stuff that life is made up of.

While one person can do it, raising kids is much easier with two people. Each person can fill a different role. One parent might be the nurturer, and the other the disciplinarian. One parent might pay for the food, and the other makes the food. One might be the smart one, and the other one the 6'2", gangly, doofus who likes watching football, comedies and writing blogs.

If it is nice to have a second parent around as back up with regular kids, it is extra nice with autistic kids. Maybe not when they are little, but definitely when they are teenagers.

(For the single moms and dads out there raising autistic children the fact that it is taking two of us to do what you are doing alone is not an indictment of you but of us. I take my hat off to the single parents doing it alone and say "Bravo" to you. I truly don't know how you do it.)

She needs you to do the thankless jobs that she cannot get to. She needs a slave/servant, and that's where you come in. Now when/if you help, here is where the twist comes in:

Sometimes it will not sound like she wants your help. She does.

Sometimes she will say she does not need your help. She does.

Don't expect her to say "Thank you" for you doing something for her that she has done for years for you, without you saying "Thank you."

Sometimes she may resent having to ask for your help, but that is part of being a modern human.

We are taught that asking for help is a sign of weakness. This is not true. Everyone needs help from time to time. Ever been to the doctor? That is a request for help. Think you can do it on your own? Ok, next time you get sick, why don't you whip up your own antibiotic from scratch. Too hard? Fine. Just mix up your own Dayquil, it can't be that hard, it only costs 4 bucks at the store.

And if you have never, ever been sick, or had to ask for help, just wait, you will. Disease and death come for us all.

Having a physically strong but mentally disabled kid, who is bigger than you, only sleeps six hours a night, and can tear doors off their hinges would be overwhelming for anyone.

Your wife needs you around once in a while, if only to remind your son that there is someone in this house still bigger, meaner, smellier and hairier than him, who despite his baseball card collection, is still the alpha male and ready to defend his territory.

She wants you, for your body. Just not the way you thought she did. Surprise!

There are ways you can help. Several weeks a year I babysit. Babysitting is caring for children. The definition is not connected to whether the children are your own or not. Even though my wife says it is not the correct definition of the term, I say, I am babysitting…my own children. For a week. Twice a year. For no pay. Yeah, I already picked a place on my mantel for my future Nobel Peace prize; excuse me while I go get some wax for my cross.

Her last trip she traveled home to Sri Lanka. The fact that the kids were off from school while she was gone was just coincidence (or was it?).

We take separate vacations. I know, like a lot of things we do, it's weird. It is an imperfect (and hopefully temporary) solution for an imperfect situation. Vacationing with my son is not a vacation. We do it from time to time, and it can be interesting, but it is definitely not relaxing or a break. It is a constant battle to keep him happy when he is out of his routine. If he is going to stay up all night breaking stuff, I would rather he do it in a place where I can afford the stuff being broken, like my crappy apartment. There is nothing at our place that has not passed the "JJ Test" and been replaced.

The tested item can be:

1. Thrown (on purpose)

2. Dropped (on accident)

3. Jumped on

4. Jumped on with a pogo stick

5. Hit with a stick/bat

6. Run over with a scooter/bike

7. Peed on

8. Thrown in the bath (if it's electronic)

9. Thrown in the toilet (if it's valuable or a toothbrush)

10. Filled with strawberry jelly (if it's electronic and has a place to put jam in it (i.e., a VCR, DVD, or CD player)

11. Filled with cake (if it is a shoe he likes)

12. All of the above

(In case you're wondering, he has in fact, taken all of the above actions against helpless items I have paid for.)

We have not been able to find someone to watch our son for a week for a long time (can't imagine why based on the above list), so it has come to this. For years we said if we couldn't go together we just won't go, so we all got to stay home and mope around together. No more.

We do unusual (or outlandish) vacations on the cheap. And save money for them by making sacrifices other ways. We rent a small apartment, share an eight-year-old car, don't have cable, and heat our place entirely on pig farts. It's totally worth it.

So for a few weeks a year, I am a single dad. Trying to balance cleaning up, work emails, expense reports, more cleaning up, working out, wiping bottoms, more cleaning up, making dinner, trips to the laundromat, work, and more cleaning up. Did I mention cleaning up?

He can make a 45-minute mess in 2 minutes flat. It's a skill. I'm thinking of renting him out to the good people at OxiClean to get the tough stains IN.

Now that they have remade *Footloose*, *Arthur*, and *Planet of the Apes*, *Mr. Mom* can't be far behind. (If you know someone, who knows someone, who knows someone who is remaking it, tell him or her I would be great for the Jack Butler character, but am also totally willing to play the Jeffrey Tambor part.)

Doing it solo is no easy task.

If you are looking for a good deed this week, help out a single parent who is drowning. Offer to mow their grass, make them a meal, or watch their kid. And remember guys--it counts as babysitting, even if the kid is also yours.

The last time I babysat, I had to buy my son a new bed. The last one was starting to come apart. Apparently it was not designed to have a 160-pound, crazy strong autistic boy jump on it every day for multiple years.

I have said many times that IKEA would do well to send us their products first for testing before selling them. We would submit them to testing that is much more rigorous than they can even imagine.

I got him a bigger, stronger bed, mattress and some shelves. It was from IKEA, so it took time to assemble. I know people complain about IKEA instructions, but I love putting the stuff together. It feels like Legos for grown ups.

After taking apart the old bed, carrying it down three flights of stairs, then carrying the new bed and mattress up those same three flights of stairs and assembling it, I had burned a few hours.

I commented to the wife, wryly, "He will never know how much of a pain this was". It was a joke, but the underlying feeling was, he can't appreciate how much time, effort, and money I put into trying to improve his life.

However, that is not only true of autistic kids; it is just true of any kids. I was thinking about all the times my Dad came out to see me play basketball. Or the special shoes he agreed to buy me to help my vertical leap. (FYI, I can still dunk… on a 9-foot rim). Or the times my mom drove me to the hospital when I tried to do a stunt that would have been perfectly at home on the TV show *Jackass*.

Part of parenting is doing the unsung things that smooth out the bumps on the roads our kids travel.

There is a trainer at my new gym named Lou Del Valle. He was the first man to ever knock down Roy Jones, Jr. (In a fight Lou went on to lose). Now he is a trainer. Today he was working with a young guy in the ring allowing the guy to throw punches while he blocked, deflected and absorbed blows. The idea is that providing a young fighter with a live target will prepare him for a real fight. He will know what it is like to hit someone, while Lou takes the brunt of the abuse.

I'm not sure the young man understood that a former World Champion was allowing himself to be hit for his benefit. That is what parenting is like. You stand in there and take a beating to better your kid's life in some way. You hope that they appreciate it; however, even if they don't, you know they benefit from the sacrifices you are making.

Here is to Lou, and everyone like him, who help others by giving a little of themselves. If I could tell a younger Kirk something it would be to say thank you to the *Lous* in your life.

Oh, and JJ has a new bed…to destroy.

Jump away, JJ. Jump away.

CHOSE HAPPINESS

There are worse places to live than NYC. For one thing, it is a great place to do stand up.

One of the reasons I love doing stand-up in NYC are the "Pop-ins." Well-known people just "pop in." This week in NYC, Louis CK and Chris Rock are both doing the rounds. A few weeks ago, Robin Williams also did a set downtown. Yes, that Robin Williams. (I know. I didn't think he did standup any more either.)

Last night I was waiting to go on stage, and I started talking to a comedian named Modi who had just gotten off stage. There was a little small talk and then he introduced me to his friend James. I said, "Nice to meet you," and we chatted a little. Modi had asked me how my autistic son was doing. James jumped in with a well thought out comment about some of the research into autism that was happening right now. He looked familiar, but I could not place him.

Thinking he might be a comedian I asked, "You going up?" (Shop-talk for, "Are you performing?")

He laughed. "No, I don't think so. I don't think I could do it. I could do it for like 30 seconds and then I would bomb."

I still could not place him. Ok, so he is not a comedian. I tried to salvage the situation and make a guess.

"Well, I figured you were an entertainer, so maybe you started in stand up." I was grasping at straws.

He laughs, "Comedy is hard. I was on Conan this week. It made me think about the first time I was on Conan. It was 14 years ago and I was at the height of my 'doucheness'. I told these terrible, long, boring stories with no punch lines. It was terrible. After the first story, I could not hear any laughter, but I figured maybe the crowd was not mic'd up, so maybe we just couldn't hear them. Then during the second ridiculous story I told, Conan could see it was going nowhere and tried to save me.

He threw in a punch line and I could hear the roar of laughter from the crowd, which was great. But then I realized, my punch line was not going to be good as his, and I have no where to go with this story." At this point James' eyes get big and he looks horrified. I can almost feel the pain he is describing. The pain of bombing that any comedian knows. Ok, so he is in show business, but I still have no idea who he is.

He continues, "It was just a weird time for me. Everything was going so well. I was 21; Varsity Blues was coming out. What can I say? I was a douchebag."

It's the dude from Dawson's Creek. That is who it is! Now, for those of you who are like, "How do you not recognize James Van der Beek?" (I had to look up his real name), you have to remember, when Dawson's Creek was big, I was in my late 20s and have testicles, so I was not really the target demographic.

He turned out to be a nice guy. Oh, and then later that night Chris Rock showed up and did 43 minutes of new stuff, very cool. I'm guessing much of it will make it to his next special. Mr. Rock mentioned he was working on a new show. As I have gotten older, I have developed a love/ hate relationship with sitcoms. I love the jokes but hate the fact that everything gets magically resolved in half an hour. That clashes with my life experience.

Sitcoms love happy endings.

From Cheers to Charles in Charge, Different Strokes, Family Matters, to the archetype for all sitcoms- Cosby Show (who would have thought this fine show would eventually birth "That's so Raven"), where every issue gets resolved in 30 minutes. (I did not see many of these shows until I was older and they were in syndication.)

The few shows I did see at the time were at my friend Joe's house. I would go over to his house, his dad worked for the consulate. He would get packages from the US. In those packages there would be 6-hour tapes someone had recorded off of broadcast TV. Six hours, commercials and all.

We would get to see not only shows we had never heard of, but also the cereals that looked delicious but were non-existent in Latin America circa 1987. My mom made her own granola, partially explaining my nuttiness (Hey-oh).

To me, the best sitcom of all time is the Cosby Show. There was an issue. Thirty minutes later, problem solved. Love it. Taking responsibility? Solved. Stealing? Solved. Staying in school? Solved.

Although it would be a nice if all my problems were solved within 30 minutes of their being divulged, that has not been my experience.

I talked to an old friend yesterday. And as it always does, the conversation eventually got to my son.

Him: So what are you going to do?

Me: No idea.

Him: What is the solution?

Me: (laughing) Solution? I don't see a solution.

It seems that way for many of us. There is no concise, sitcom like, solution.

If the Cosby Show covered autism, it might play out like this:

1. JJ, the autistic neighbor kid, is introduced.
2. Dr. Huxtable, being a doctor, decides to start working at a lab to find a cure for autism.
3. Dr. Huxtable finds said cure in 30 minutes of TV time, all the while delivering jokes.
4. Dr. Huxtable makes some faces at the end and does a little dance. Yahoo.

I have to be honest. It sounds great. I love it. It would work. Bill (we are on a first name basis) is a great comedian and would make it work. It would be a great show. I would watch it again and again.

But...that is not how most of our lives are. Things are unresolved. Sometimes it is our fault; sometimes things are just un-resolvable. There are things undone or unsaid that are only that way because of our own timidity, laziness or fear. There are other problems that are not "fixable" in this lifetime. But there can be a beautiful story unfolding around the flaws of our lives.

(And I say this last part to myself, most of all.)

Don't dissect the pearl in order to thoroughly inspect the grain of sand.

Focus on the pearl not the irritant.

Don't allow the present problems to poison your appetite to the delectable wonders you encounter everyday.

Don't choose a life of quiet desperation.

Being in show business (even at the cusp like I am) is the exact opposite of being with a disabled person.

While celebrities yearn for privacy, a disabled person (or their family) can hide in plain sight.

Sometimes I feel invisible.

The easiest way to hide in plain sight is to be down and out, deprived, or disabled. As a family, we know what it is like to be uninvited to parties, events, and churches. Rules are different for those who don't easily fit into society's box of what it means to be normal.

If you are rich and powerful everyone wants a piece of you.

People listen to your advice. You can be an ignoramus spewing gibberish, but if you're a billionaire ignoramus, when you speak, people will nod respectfully and call you eccentric. Try to pontificate to those same people while dressed as a homeless person, smelling of gin and urine. People will literally sprint away from you. You'll see chubby people move like you did not know they could. The nice ones will throw change at you as they run.

The labels change the more money and power you have. As a woman, if you sleep around and you're rich, you're a "free sprit" with a flair for the "bohemian life style" who does not "play by society's rules". If you're poor and sleep around, you're a slag, hussy, or slut.

What do you call someone who does not have a cell phone or wallet, doesn't know how to drive, and has no plans to work this month? It depends on the decimal in his bank account. He is either very, very poor or very, very rich. If he is the latter, he is welcomed everywhere, all of his sins are overlooked. The former isn't even invited to his family's house for the holidays.

The situation with my son is complicated, making things hard to plan. When we go to someone's house, he could be good. Which means, playing with his toys, or watching a video on a portable DVD player. Or he could be bad, which means crying for some unknown reason or insisting on getting naked. These are hard things for people to get their heads around; I understand that. For that reason, we are not invited to many events.

However, people are living poorer lives excluding the disabled and infirm. Being around these people reminds us of their own mortality and of the frailty of the human body and mind. These are good things to remember. We live richer, fuller lives when we are reminded of the tenuousness of it all. It could all be taken from you. The ability to walk, think, and dress yourself are not universal, eternal guarantees. Sickness and death come to us all. As connected as you are to life, you will be connected to death.

We don't expect our friends to cure JJ. We just want to connect with others, like everyone else; like my son wants to do, in his own unique way. The point and beauty of community is not that it alleviates the pain, but it allows us to not go through the pain alone, delivering a measure of joy to all involved. It is bittersweet, a microcosm for all of life.

I love to be happy, but is it possible that happiness is overrated? C.S Lewis said:

> If you think of this world as a place intended simply for our happiness, you find it quite intolerable; think of it as a place of training and correction and it's not so bad. [v]

This is advice I would give to a younger me:

Try to be happy.

Chose to be happy.

But chose to not *pursue* happiness.

Happiness is important to us. As a culture we are taught to search for happiness. The framers of the constitution even put it in the document, "the pursuit of happiness" right after "life" and "liberty." I understand "life" and "liberty", it's "the pursuit of happiness" that confounds me. I think they meant it as the freedom to choose your life's calling because pursuing happiness does not seem to bring happiness.

The more happiness is pursued, the more elusive it becomes. Nothing is sadder than a grown man pursuing happiness at any cost. The reason so many kids were raised without a father is because their dads were out chasing things they thought would make them happy.

People are chasing something that does not be need to be chased. Happiness does not need to be chased. It needs to be chosen.

We don't need to be miserable human beings. Pursue the things you enjoy, just not at everyone else's expense.

To pursue our own happiness at the expense of our fellow humans is a recipe for human misery. (You ARE your brother's keeper.)

Choose happiness. Happiness is always the journey, never the destination.

When you least expect it, happiness will find you. Where and when you least expect it, happiness will overwhelm you, coming from a place you considered running from. Aren't you glad you didn't hide from it?

PEOPLE ARE PEOPLE

We moved a lot when I was a kid, sowing in me wanderlust to see everything this world has to offer. After dreaming of China for years, I went to Beijing last year for the first time.

There is a meal in China called Hot Pot. It is prepared at your table. It's basically a boiling pot of water that you stick food into for a few minutes then you take the food out and eat it. In the US, it would be a lawsuit waiting to happen.

I had it the second night I was there. It was terrible. I mean really bad. Like eating a mushy diaper bad. The night before I left, I had it again by accident. I was wandering around trying to find the Kung Fu Theater, and I wandered into a restaurant. In front of the restaurant there was a guy heating coals with some sort of home made sanding belt that was sending sparks all over. I recognized the Hot Pots on the table, but was running out of time and could not find any other restaurant in the area.

The place was packed, which is usually a really good sign. Often, if I am in a new place and I don't know where to go, I get in line. Usually there is a reason so many people are in line. The collective intelligence of the group is higher than any one individual. Especially if that individual is me…and I am lost…in a place where I don't speak the language.

The menu was entirely in Chinese except for the numbers. Oh boy. I wanted chicken. I tried saying chicken. Nothing. Then I tried saying it louder, like we Americans like to do. Nothing. Then I turned to charades and acted like a chicken-both thumbs under my armpits, arms flapping up and down--like I was at a wedding doing the chicken dance. I jutted my head back and forth like San Francisco 49er Merton Hanks after scoring a touch down.

I danced around the restaurant like a chicken. I danced some more. They are laughing a lot but still not getting it.

The waitress calls out the cooks from the kitchen and they are laughing and talking. Slowly the restaurant seems to grind to a halt as people turn to look.

How can they not get it? I am nailing this. I finally stop, sweating, hands on my hips.

Then the waitress tells me in English, "You want chicken, ok, no ploblem. (sic) I wanted to see how long you'd dance."

I guess, some places they don't speak English. Some places they do. But, either way, a goofball doing the chicken dance is hard to pass up.

After dinner (which was great, by the way), I made it to the theater. I saw the Beijing Kung Fu show. Terrific. It was Cirque du Soleil meets *Enter the Dragon* only with more yelling and singing.

If you get the chance, both things are a "can't miss" in Beijing.

The Hot Pot meal made me think what a difference it makes when something is done right. The first version was terrible. It wasn't really hot, and the ingredients were not up to par. If I had not had it that second time I would have thought I hated Hot Pot. But I actually hated a bad version of Hot Pot. I wonder how many other things I have written off because I experienced a bad copy of them.

Sometimes I think I do myself a disservice by not giving things a chance. If I had judged the Kung Fu show by the Kung Fu "demonstration" we had at our junior high by a person seemingly ripped from the world of *Napoleon Dynamite*, I would have missed out on one of the highlights of the trip.

Dancing around the restaurant I thoroughly embarrassed myself, but I am trying to get to the point where I don't worry about the judgments of others. I just try to be myself.

When I first found out my son was disabled, I felt shame from time to time. If I could talk to myself when I was 24 and first found out about my son's condition, I would tell myself:

You feel some shame for your son's condition. Don't. There is no shame in being disabled.

This should be obvious, but it is not.

I had an interesting discussion about shame with a friend. She talked of feeling shame. She suffered through an illness and now there are things she can no longer do physically.

Society has conditioned us to feel shame if we deviate at all from the status quo we see in the media. If you don't look like Megan Fox or George Clooney, you should be a little embarrassed. But if you, God forbid, become disabled through an accident or illness, you should feel shame. Not sadness over loss, but out and out shame.

You're disabled? You should hide.

You should tell no one.

Don't open up to others about what you are going through.

Life is always grand; we never go through any difficult times.

And my least favorite bit of advice: Fake it 'till you make it.

I understand where it comes from, trying to be positive. But if you fake it and never make it, you're just a faker. Nice advice. Just lie to everyone, and most importantly, to yourself, forever. Great.

When I look around and see people with giant Cheshire cat grins on their faces, I always wonder: Real or replica? Blissful or bitter?

People feel shame in disability when they should not. You should not feel shame for being something you did not chose. It is what it is.

Why do we suffer in pain, silently? Alone. Quieted by the shame. Why do we feel shame at all for suffering from a disability we did not chose?

You don't (and shouldn't) feel shame about your height, bone structure, skin color, or race. Things you didn't decide. No one chooses disability.

In that way, my son is lucky. He does not have society's baggage to deal with. I don't think shame is something he struggles with. He has no shame in being who he is.

He could run through a Wal-Mart, butt naked, screaming and feel no shame. (Being Wal-Mart, no one would even give him a second look. Come on people, it's Wal-Mart).

Oh to be like my son and feel no shame.

When I was his age, I was easily embarrassed. Having spent my childhood in places people knew so little about, there were bound to be questions and I was always embarrassed by people's lack of knowledge.

First question and answer, "No, Ecuador is not all jungle." We Americans know very little about geography and many times ask the most uninformed questions. When people ask me dumb questions, I can't help but give them dumb answers.

Some of my favorite questions I have been asked about Ecuador:

Are there car crashes in Ecuador? Yes, there are car crashes, but we fill all our cars with candy, so when they crash, they explode like piñatas.

Do you have jails in Ecuador? Jails? No, we just send all our convicts to our penal colony called Queens.

Did you live under a tree? Under a tree? No. In a tree? Yeah. We were like the Swiss family Robinson, except less clever inventions and more diarrhea.

What part of Mexico is Ecuador in? The part without hot sauce, Chiclets, or Mexicans.

Do you speak Mexican? Yes, and Australian, New Zealandish, Cuban, and American.

In Ecuador, we lived in Guayaquil, a city of several million. It's not what most people think of when they think of Ecuador, Guayaquil is far from the jungle. I have been out to the Amazon jungle a couple of times. The last time I went out there I got Dengue Fever. Not fun. And not at all like Jungle Fever.

I put bug spray over every inch of my skin that was exposed. Part of the trip involved a canoe ride during which I hunched over and the back of my shirt came up a little, exposing a bit of lower back skin where some women get tattoos. A mosquito proceeded to bite me several dozen times leaving me with a pattern of welts that looked like I had been spanked. Then I got Dengue Fever. Joint pain and exhaustion were the symptoms I remember most. Its duration: weeks and weeks of being too tired to even watch TV. Edward R. Murrow said the opiate of the masses was TV, not religion or alcohol, the small screen. When Americans are feeling sick their medicine of choice is the boob tube.

There was never much on TV in Ecuador. There were only three local broadcast channels. We did not even get a TV until I was 10. And when we did, there was never much on those three local channels.

I missed giant chunks of American TV and culture. There are entire fads and TV series that I missed. When I moved back to the US, nothing made me feel more left out than when something would come up that I had missed entirely. Someone would say:

"Hey, remember on the A-Team, when Murdock would try to trick BA into flying by putting a roofie in his drink, and then he would wake up all mad and be like, 'I pity the fool'." "Oh, remember on Different Strokes, when Willis would try to tell Arnold what to do, and Arnold would be like 'Whatchu talkin' 'bout Willis?'"

I would have no idea what *they* were talking about. My knowledge of that time was totally different. What I would want to say would be:

"Oh yeah, the late 80's. Remember when inflation in Ecuador was running at 50% so at the end of the year your money was worth half what it was at the beginning of the year. And the squares at the IMF were like 'you need to control your spending', and Ecuador was like 'whatever', and then the IMF was like 'if you default, we will cut you off' and Ecuador was like, 'Whatchu talkin' 'bout Willis?'"

However, that never got me laughs. Just vacant stares, wedgies or swirlies.

One of the few American shows we did get was badly dubbed MacGyver episodes. Which makes total sense. I think MacGyver was first generation Mexican American. Think about it. He can fix anything with just duct tape, he travels with just a backpack and he has a mullet. I am convinced if you searched his person you would find Chiclets.

Joking aside, I would tell my younger self. People are just people. Some are famous, some anonymous, some rich, some poor, some powerful, and some powerless. But we are all basically the same.

Met Martin Freeman once, we had coffee at the same café in front of the Globe Theater in London. The British Office is my favorite show of all time so Freeman is my hero but I have to tell you. I met him. He is just a dude. We try to divide people up by race, religion or skills but they are just that, people. There is more that unites us that divides us. Focus on building bridges not burning them. You will be surprised by where your allies come from.

DREAM BIG

My first taste of Latin American was when I was five. My parents wanted to preach to the unsaved masses, and after some planning we were off.

Like most American kids at age five, I barely spoke English. The first country we moved to was El Salvador where they speak Spanish. I didn't speak a single word of it, but I learned.

I think one of my best attributes is my willingness to make an absolute fool of myself. I do get embarrassed, but I don't consider that a good enough reason not to try something.

The best way to learn a language is to immerse yourself in the culture and launch out in conversation. Try. Don't worry about syntax or grammar. Do it. Pronounce the words the best you can. Try to communicate. People will correct you. They will laugh at you (and belittle you to their friends), but they will correct you, and that is how you will learn. The sting from their laughter will make you focus. You will remember that lesson and move on to the next one.

El Salvador's civil war in the 1980s meant there was not much to do that was considered safe. One thing we could do on Saturday was go to one of the Western hotels, pay a couple of bucks, and swim in their pool.

When I was six, I remember being at a hotel pool with my mom and two brothers. As we ate lunch, I made a mess and needed a napkin. My mom, not a coddler, told me to go get one. I walked over to a find a waiter and asked for a "servilleta."

The waiter looked at me funny. I repeated it, "Dos servilletas, por favor." He repeated it back to me. I said "Si," and with all of the authority I could muster at six, tried to look serious, "Si, dos servilletas por favor."

He came back with "dos *cervezas*" (two beers) and asked me where I wanted to put them.

Ok, "servilletas" (napkins) and "cervezas" (beers) are pretty close. Put them over there. My mom disagreed and had them returned.

"Servilleta" is different than "cerveza." Lesson learned. Second lesson? They don't card in El Salvador.

From El Salvador we moved to Costa Rica.

Costa Rica was great. My most vivid memory is riding my bike, with no hands, hitting a rock, and ending up trying to grind gravel into my face.

My poor mom had to, once again, take me to the emergency room and have me patched up like a slightly bigger Raggedy Ann. I was sure the six stitches over my eye would make me look tough. If not like the guy from *Valhalla Rising*, at least it would look a little bit like the scar Inigo Montoya sported.

"My name is Kirk Smith. You killed my father, prepare to die."

The scar ended up mostly in my eyebrow, and within a year or two, it was hardly visible. I was once again no more menacing than a prepubescent Mr. Rogers.

From there we moved to Ecuador in 1985.

Ecuador is a beautiful country and for the last several years has been the top foreign destination for American retirees. The mountain towns have a well-deserved reputation for excellent weather, low cost of living, and good medical care. All the retirees move to the mountains, usually Cuenca at 8500 ft. Cuenca, with its year-round highs at 70F, safe cobblestone streets, and thermal baths, is arguably a paradise.

However we lived on the coast. Far from the 70-degree daily highs in Cuenca, Guayaquil's high was in the low 200's with humidity that makes Houston seem like San Francisco. The old jokes were:

It's where the devil comes to get away from the heat. Or, it was so hot your junk would stick to someone else's leg.

When people would come to visit Guayaquil, they would immediately want to go visit the mountains, and we could take them. We had a 1979 Chevy Blazer. It had three forward gears that you would need to double clutch to find. After learning to drive on that, everything else seemed like cheating. "What do you mean you don't have to put in the clutch, take it out of gear, rev the engine, and try to match the rpm's to the road speed before getting it into gear? Next you are going to tell me there are phones that you can take out of your car and also watch movies on them."

At the time there were three of us biological kids and an 18-year-old young man, Paco, who was staying with us for a bit.

His parents had been killed in a car accident and he was in a tough spot. He was to stay with us his last year of high school before going off to make his mark on the world. From the look of things, his mark was going to be on women. He was a natural charmer. He had a way of putting women at ease…and we learned later, easing them out of their clothes.

Most of his time at home he spent in front of the mirror, asking me, in the only English sentence he knew, "Do I look too skinny?" He did, but I would say, "Oh, no. The weights are totally paying off." Paco was playing semi-pro soccer and was obviously quite athletic. Me? Not so much. We were both lifting weights; not that you could tell. The only thing the weights seemed to do for me was remind me how little of them I could lift. They would sit in a stack and taunt me with their pound and metric amounts stenciled on them like cheap temporary tattoos compensating for a lack of attention. Was I the only one who noticed that 45 pounds does not equal 25 kg? Does no one care about math?

Paco and I shared a room and were close. Probably not the best idea for a 13 year old to learn about life from a womanizing 18 year old, but there you have it. Paco and I would travel the city on the bus, and I would try to learn how to be cool. It didn't really work.

Busses in Ecuador do not slow down for men to get on or off. When a bus is picking you up, in an effort to save time and brakes (or in a display of driver laziness) it does not stop, it only slows. Slows enough for you to run along side and hop on. When you are ready to get off, it is the same. It does not stop for you, if you have testicles. It merely slows. It is like a line graph chart. When the road speed slows enough to reach where it intersects your manliness, you jump. If it slows too much, the driver will tell you, "Jump you fairy." Some guys can jump off at around 15 miles an hour. It's pretty cool to watch. Now, here comes the important part that I learned, like most lessons, the hard way.

Always lead with your outside (right) foot. If you lead with your left foot, your momentum will carry you forward, crossing your legs and flattening you out on the side of the road. I learned this lesson in rush hour, on the busiest street in Guayaquil.

Paco and I made our way to the front of the packed bus to get off. To exit we were going to have to pass by two very pretty girls. Paco took the lack of space between him and the first girl as a chance to say something witty and give her the eye. She laughed. As I approached the two women, I tried to think of something clever to say. As it turned out, it was not needed, as I stepped on the first woman's feet with my size 13 shoes and she yelled and pushed me.

Paco got to the front and very nimbly jumped off when it seemed like the bus was doing 90 miles an hour. I was going to be just a step behind him. Sure I was 13 and my coordination hadn't kicked in, but what could go wrong?

As I jumped off the last step of the bus I felt the wind in my hair and immediately realized, this is not going to end well.

I led with my left foot and planted it firm. I tried to pull my right leg out from behind my left leg but it didn't work. The world slowed down like in the cartoons and I tried to get my hands out in front of me. The cup I had in my hand went flying. My hands and face met the pavement almost at the same time. I half rolled to my left, seeing the bus tires pass inches from my face. I looked up and saw what I was sure was all of Guayaquil looking down at me bleeding, and the two very pretty girls laughing. Paco turned to me, and in a voice that everyone could hear said, "Why did you do that?"

Why? Oh 'cause, I like flattening myself in front of strangers. It's all part of my meticulously planned out strategy. Yep, it was all part of my plan for world domination. Step one, face plant from a moving bus in front of an entire city. Step two, invade Poland.

From then on, I always exited the bus with my right foot.

On one occasion, we had a couple visiting us from the states, and they wanted to see the mountain paradise.

The Blazer fit five people and their luggage relatively comfortably; six miserably, and there were eight of us. It was decided (not by me) that Paco and I would take the bus up to the mountains and meet up with the family there.

This was in the 80s when bus travel in Ecuador meant traveling with live chickens and livestock, as well as deodorant-less passengers. Among my many psychoses is my aversion to bad odor. I don't know if this trip is where its roots stem from, but I despise few things as much as being pressed up against someone who smells like onions, death, or dysentery.

Upon getting on the bus, Paco practically sprinted to the seat next to the one young woman closest to our age. In any other circumstance, she would have been slightly above average, but here, among this motley crew who looked like they spent their days being beaten with Ugly sticks, she was a goddess.

I looked around at the few empty seats remaining and saw a sweet looking older lady and sat down. I immediately knew it was a mistake. The smell was overwhelming. After catching a whiff, if you had asked me for odds on whether we would find a dead rodent on her person, I would have given you 2 to 1.

I tried to breathe short breaths through my mouth and was sure I was going to die. I was getting dizzy. It was either the odor, or the short breaths that were making me hyperventilate.

Squinting through my now burning eyes, I looked to see Paco and the girl laughing. Great. He has another girlfriend, and I'm sitting next to the personification of death and dying.

I could see my tombstone now:

Kirk Smith: Died by asphyxiation at 13. His biggest regret was not ever having sex or even really having kissed a girl…unlike Paco.

Ok, Kirk. Fight through the burning. Look around. Is there another empty seat? My eyes focused in time to see the last open seat taken by someone else. Oh boy.

I looked over at my seatmate and meekly smiled, eyebrows raised, eyes wide open, like a madman. At this age trying to look natural always made me look like a manic--trying to hide his ear collection by smiling too big and making eye contact for too long. Or opening with something too personal or irrelevant.

"Nice to meet you. I really like cereal." Ok, psycho.

I settled into my seat and tried to regulate my breathing. I can't pass out or she'll drag me to her smelly lair.

I closed my eyes and tried to imagine a beautiful place. A gorgeous beach. The sound of the waves, the swaying palm trees. Wait. Why does this beach smell like a garbage truck just dropped off the byproduct of a liposuction and spoiled Durian fruit?

The smell pulled me back to the present snapping me wide-awake. There was a new smell. Corn. My diminutive companion had pulled from her bag of death a piece of maize or "choclo." Not the sweet corn we get in the states, but a knobby, hard little piece of corn. The kind of corn that looked like it would have been rejected even from one of those famers markets in Brooklyn where the vegetables look like they were part of a post apocalyptic harvest.

As she brought the cob to her mouth and parted her lips, her six remaining teeth were revealed. Her lack of teeth did little to dissuade her current pursuit. She attacked that piece of reject corn like it owed her money. Her six teeth's lack of uniformity meant the kernels were not being removed systematically, but wildly. Sure, some of the kernels were making it into her mouth; but some ended up on the floor, some on her lap, some on my lap, some in the hair of the lady sitting in front of us. She picked the kernels up from her lap, my lap, my arm, and the other lady's hair. Given the amount of kernels she picked off my lap, that little Indian lady owes me money.

I have never been able to hide what I'm thinking. I am such a simple man that I am not even able to fool myself, making me the worst poker player ever. Good cards, big smile. Bad cards, anger and slapping them down on the table. Even when I have good cards but pretend to have bad cards, I cannot help but to impishly smile as I throw them down on the table.

Apparently my face, despite my best effort, showed my amazement at what was happening just next to me. The lady, who must have been suffering from cataracts, interpreted my shock and horror as interest.

"You want some choclo?"

"What? No thank you."

"Are you sure? No choclo?"

Am I sure I don't want you to reach into your little bag of death, wrap your dirty little hand around a piece of mangled corn so I too can riddle the floor with its remnants? Yeah, I'm sure.

"Oh well, more for me." And sure enough, another equally mangled ear came out to have its kernels end up mostly on my lap.

Thankfully, after five ears of corn and a tomato, we arrived in the mountain town of Baños.

I suffer from altitude sickness. The first few days when I'm up that high exercise is out of the question, and I get headaches. My mind slows and my speech becomes somewhat slurred. Put me above 8000 feet for a few days and I sound like a drunk who hides it rather well. There is, however, a great side effect to the altitude sickness: dreams. The dreams are more vivid than the kind you get by eating walnuts and pickles immediately before going to bed. These are lucid alternate universes where the unimaginable feels not only true, but also obvious. I dream that I am a rabbit farmer who becomes rich when one of my rabbits begins to speak. The rabbit speaks only in Latin. And as Latin is no longer a spoken language, we soon learn from the rabbit that we are saying it all wrong. The rabbit goes on to fame and fortune, and I am left telling incredulous souls that I knew the rabbit way back when, here on the farm, when his name was just Pepe.

I once dreamt that I had a wife and a girlfriend, and I decided the best course of action would be to have them live in the same house. I somehow thought they would not ever run into each other and spent my days trying to make sure their paths did not cross. Like a loopy Faulty Towers character.

Another time I dreamt that I was peeing blood, and in that dream, I nodded and lifted my eyebrows as an acknowledgement of the inevitable. The dreams are not particularly interesting in their content but their vividness, realness and their feeling of inevitability always make me look forward to sleeping in the mountains.

But back to the story at hand. Our visiting friends spoke little Spanish. The few words they did speak were often mispronounced and out of context.

Learning a new language is hard enough but there was another small wrinkle to add to our moves around Latin America. All of the Latin American countries are a little different, and all have a few words that they don't share or that have different meanings.

A straw in El Salvador is called a "pajilla"; in Ecuador it is called a "sorbete", which is the same word used for ice cream in El Salvador. More than once, in Ecuador, I have accidently said; I don't need an "ice cream" for my drink, which makes people nod as if to say, "obviously."

In Ecuador the word for bag or sack is "funda", in El Salvador its "bolsa". In Ecuador, "bolsa" means scrotum or *ball* sack.

In Ecuador they love to use the word "cojer", which means to grab or pick up. In Argentina the same word is the f-word. What a difference 20 degrees of southern latitude can make.

There are also words in Spanish that sound like English words but have different meanings. We call them false friends. In Spanish the word "embarasado" sounds like "embarrassed", but it means pregnant.

It can be a little confusing. If you forget your shopping bag in a store and come back to get it, don't accidently say, "I am so pregnant that I forgot my scrotum." People will look at you funny.

A friend of mine who speaks at schools for a living came down to do some presentations. He tried to ask several groups of kids how old they were. He thought he was saying "Cuantos años tienes?" but actually said, "Cuanto anus tienes?" or "How many anuses do you have?" Not exactly the same question. He was wondering why people would laugh when he asked. We told him what he was doing…three days later after he had asked hundreds of people about the number of anuses they possessed. He asked why we took so long to tell him. We told him the truth; it was just too good pass up. (This was the same guy who told the story of Jonah spending 3 days in a "vajina" (vagina) instead of "ballena" (whale). Not exactly the same story.)

Not knowing the language or where you are going can cause some strange developments. In Ecuador if you ask someone where something is and they don't know, often they are too embarrassed to say as much. Ask for directions on how to get somewhere in much of Ecuador and people will give them to you. The fact that they have no idea where the place you want to go is located, rarely stops them. They want to be helpful. You seem nice. What can be the harm in giving the man some directions? Any directions?

"Uhh, yeah, you want to go down that way south, for about 4 blocks, then turn left."

"I was just down there. They sent me here."

"Oh, yeah. Right. In that case, yeah, go north 5 blocks and turn right."

If they have no idea where it is, they will make an impassioned plea about where you should look for it. In fact, the conviction they feel about where they should send you is directly correlated to their lack of knowledge about its location. If they have no idea where it is, they will practically scream the directions at you.

"I am SURE. I would swear on my dog's grave, it is 5 BLOCKS NORTH AND THEN TURN RIGHT...I MEAN LEFT."

It is not just Ecuadorians who give mixed messages in Ecuador. Americans are equally as good at it.

The Douglases, our visitors, were a couple from Kentucky who moved to Ecuador and brought their dog Penny (which they pronounced "pee-nee") with them. "Pene" means penis in Spanish. Some times the dog would get out of the house and they would have to go looking for it.

Nothing would make me and my brother laugh harder than seeing Mrs. Douglas out wandering the streets, yelling for "pene" at the top of her lungs. She eventually found her dog but not before getting her share of winks and catcalls.

Not having a shared language can present other problems.

Recently, while staying in a hotel in Ecuador, some friends of mine had an eventful night.

At 3 am, someone from the front desk knocked on their door, came in their room, looked around, said "mas frio", turned their air-conditioning down a little and left. Now the worker did not speak English, and the guys in the room did not speak Spanish. After the employee left the room without another word, my friends just looked at each other like, "Huh?"

They had lots of questions. How does the hotel monitor the temperature in each room? Do they also advise you on your water temperature when showering? And how do they determine what is cool enough for each guest? Is the decision based on any other factors besides the clerk's discretion?

They tried to ask what happened in the morning but the language barrier was too high. So I talked to the manager to see what had happened. It turns out there was a fire alarm going off in one of the rooms. The employee ended up going to the wrong room and once there, he did not know what to say on account of the linguistic challenge. So he decided to go with, "mas frio" which is the shorten version of " we are going to all the rooms and making sure their air conditioners are cool enough…at 3 am. You're welcome."

The moral of the story being, if you end up in the wrong hotel room in the middle of the night, yell something incoherent in Spanish and exit.

That was a fun trip, and my family was able to travel with me on this one. We do try to all travel together at least once a year. I know the kids are growing up, and I know my daughter will eventually moving out.

You are cared for at the beginning of your life and at the end of your life, but in the middle, hopefully, you are independent for a good 50 years. That is what you hope for. It does not look like that is going to happen for my son, although there are moments when actions spark in me the belief, if only for a moment, that it is possible.

I saw a glimmer of hope when my son learned to ride a bike last year. He was 13. I bought him a bike at Christmas, again. It's the fourth one we've bought him. Normally his first step is to flip it over and spin the wheels, turning them into spinning "looms" where he can stick random objects in and watch them be shot off like little kids on a merry-go-round.

Step number two is where he tries to dismantle it. Within a few months we usually have what looks like a bike graveyard. Where good bikes come to die.

This time, however, he rode it several times with training wheels and he seemed to be getting the hang of it. He hunched over like he was really concentrating, focusing all his energies on his bike. Then one day, while he was riding, one of the training wheels fell off and he kept going, making me want to yell, "Ride Forrest, Ride!" at the top of my lungs.

It was magical just like the movie *Forrest* Gump, where the shackles of a previous impairment fall off and he transcends the moment, vaulting him to the next level of life…just as Forrest did (but with less running and more hunching).

That first day he learned to ride, we went for a 20-minute run/bike ride. I think it was the first father/son sporting activity we had ever done. We have tried many others, unsuccessfully. It is not truly a game of catch if one of the players refuses to catch the ball, and instead lets it hit him in the face. The same goes for basketball…and football.

It really did feel like a milestone. A delayed one, but a milestone nonetheless.

Here is to growing as people, one painstakingly slow step at a time.

Within a month, I was ditched; it was inevitable. It was bound to happen. He was on a bike. I was running at age 38, and breathing as if I was going into labor.

He took off, and I was left eating his dust.

He had mastered the peddling and now was only falling over every other trip.

We were riding and running when he suddenly put his head down and started peddling furiously. He gave me a little sideways glance, a smirk, and he was off.

I started full on sprinting for the first 50 yards, but then age took over and I had to slow down. I could hear him squeal with delight as he pulled ahead. In my mind, he was like the little pig from the Geico commercials squealing and saying, "Pure adrenaline".

He left me behind.

Oh, that he would do that in life. That it would be a metaphor for all he does. That he would be better than me at riding and running, speaking and writing and living.

I think that is what everyone wants for his or her kid. That their the child would surpass all the accomplishments of the parent.

We want them to dream bigger, go farther and be wildly more successful than us. It does not have to be shown in public like this, where I am left coughing and wheezing. But it would be great if his successes, when compared to mine, left me looking like a middle-aged, out of shape man gasping for breath.

That our children would go farther and dream bigger, experiencing greater successes than I ever imagined.

The advice I would give to myself I give to my son. Dream, big boy. Dream big, boy.

Godspeed to you, which my brother says is usually 3 mph.

DON'T JUDGE BY THE COVER

In 2002 my mother-in-law became sick with cancer. She was living in Sri Lanka at the time, running an orphanage. Her diagnosis was serious, and being a Swedish national, she returned to Sweden for surgeries and treatment. My wife was naturally concerned and wanted to be at her mother's side. We had a 5 and 3 year old at the time, and had just moved from Northern California to Orange County.

We decided she should go. She packed some things and flew with the kids to Sweden.

Her mom had gone back to her hometown, which was right in the middle of the country, about three hours north of Stockholm.

What was supposed to be a trip of a few weeks turned into months. My wife wanted to stay until her mother was better, and we had no idea how long that would be. After 3 months, I transferred to my company's UK office. The idea was that I would work in the UK on the weekdays, and go to Sweden on the weekends.

Our offices were located in Swindon. Swindon means "Swine Hill," and the description is not far off. When people think of the UK, they think of London. But Swindon has very little in common with London.

The references to Swindon in the British version of *The Office* were right on the nose--a boring little factory town with little to do. The surrounding area, however, was rife with activities.

I lived in a little Anglo-Saxon town called Cricklade. It was a beautiful little town of a few thousand people. Located just above Swindon and just below the Cotswolds, this little town was the real McCoy, small stone houses centered mostly around the area of High Street which had its 6 pubs to serve the town's several thousand inhabitants.

63

The main pubs were the Red Lion, the White Lion, and the Vale. Locals clearly picked a side; a particular pub. This was Hatfield and McCoy stuff. There were very few people that would patronize all three. You had your special place, the one pub you were loyal to. Sure, you had the back up place you would go to if John Davidson, your sworn enemy, was around, and you didn't want to bump into that little git. But as a rule, you went to one of the three.

Everyone had a good reason for that, too. "I can't go to the Vail. The previous owner was a real jerk when he went to sell the pub in 1962. My cousin Ned tried to buy it, but he sold it to someone else, the tosser".

Or, "My dad got kicked out of the Red Lion for being drunk 40 years ago. What's that? Was he drunk? Yeah, he was blathered. But that's not the point, is it? I won't set foot in that place!"

I ended up mainly at the Vale. Mostly because that is where the local bishop invited us after church. I attended St. Sampson's Church, which was built in the 11th century. I did not agree with everything being said at this church, but I felt there was more that united us than divided us, so I went. After church, the minister would tell the congregation, "let's go down to the pub and fellowship", which to a kid raised Pentecostal translated, "let's go down to the pits of hell to hang out." I went.

One of the things in that church that made me most uncomfortable was not a difference of philosophy, but of hygiene. During communion, we would all drink from the same glass. Oh boy. I am a germ weirdo. I don't like to get sick. In fact, I prefer to avoid it. So as a rule, I don't like to drink after people. I certainly don't want to drink after 100 strangers, most of whom are old and infirm. I have nothing against old people. I love old people. I have old relatives. I just don't want to drink from a glass that has been touched by a 100 sets of dentures. The best thing would be to get in line at the beginning, before everyone has had a chance to add their saliva to the cup. However, in a church, it is frowned upon to push old people to the side during communion just to be first. No one knows you're a germ weirdo. They just think you're a weirdo.

There were not many people my age at this church. Though I love old people, unless you are an octogenarian, it's not healthy to have your social circle made up entirely of them, so I looked outside the church for other social outlets. I ended up joining a local rugby club.

If you know what I look like, then this funny. I am not exactly the manliest looking man. I am not small in stature (about 6'2", 180 lbs), but I have a face like a child and a tendency to laugh or smile a big goofy grin when I shouldn't.

I like sports, but am not what I would call a natural. I'm more of a grinder. Just keep practicing, and working, and grinding and eventually you will see some fruit. Probably not the results you hoped for, but something. As I mentioned before, I played college basketball, but that may have left a false impression about my athleticism. Our coach recruited several criminals who were very good athletes, and several choirboys who were not good athletes, in the hope that it would balance out. There would be a murderer, a rapist, and then me, a victim.

I would start games as punishment to other players, then someone would make bail and I would be back on the bench. I guess if I was really competitive, I could have squealed on someone to get more playing time. But it is a humbling feeling to start games as a punishment for someone else. "Kirk you're starting again. No, not as a reward for all the hard work you put in, but because someone who is more talented than you can't seem to pass an easy geology class called Rocks for Jocks. So until Steve here learns that Stone Philips is not the name of a rock, you're playing."

Conjuring up all the manliness I could muster, I joined the Cricklade Rugby Union Club (now called the Cricklade RFC).

The guys were surprisingly accepting considering my lack of knowledge, skill, and talent.

There is no way around it. The game is very physical. Think football without pads, helmets or play stoppage. Full disclosure: I am not built for contact sports like these. If you examine my body closely you'll see I am built for naps, crocheting, or perhaps light reading.

To American ears, the English accent has a type of whimsy. Most Brits sound to me like Bilbo Baggins describing the Shire. However, when my new teammates were describing what the games would be like, these same accents, by no fault of their own, failed to capture the game's violence. That was not the only time the accent led me astray.

With sports, when I analyze my abilities after the fact, I feel I get a good picture of what my deficiencies are. However, adrenaline often deludes my reality at the height of the moment.

During one of the games, I took offence at what I felt was a cheap shot while I was on the ground. I got in the guy's face and we grabbed each other's jerseys and yelling ensued. He was built like a truck, but was a good 5 inches shorter than me, and he proceeded to threaten me with very specific violence. I laughed, and taunted him some more. The thing is, he had a very thick accent (which I later learned was Cockney) and I had a very hard time understanding what he was saying. From my experience playing basketball at many urban playgrounds during my college days, the tough guys were the ones with inner-city accents, not British ones. This was before I had seen the movie *Lock, Stock, and Two Smoking Barrels*, so to me it felt like this guy was about to start reciting Shakespeare.

During the next break in the action one of my teammates said, "Careful with him."

Me: Him? (Incredulous.)

Teammate: Yeah. He just got out of jail last week.

Me: For what?

Teammate: Stabbing somebody.

Me: And they let him go?

Teammate: Bloke didn't die. He was in 4 years.

The rest of the game I continued to play hard but steered clear of Bilbo and did significantly less taunting (read, none).

After the game, we were like bosom buddies. I still could not understand what he was saying, but there was lot of laughing and backslapping going on.

After the games, we would go to the Working Man's Club, an absolute dump, where there would be various drinking games in progress. The point to all of them seemed to be who could drink the most the fastest and then put the empty glass upside-down on top of their head. And there seemed to be no correlation between playing hard, missing teeth and alcohol tolerance.

My run-in with "stabby" taught me a valuable lesson; it was hard to tell who is the real McCoy. It has taken me a long time to learn this but younger Kirk; you really can't judge a book by its cover.

DON'T COMPARE

My daughter was born in San Ramon, California (AKA Super "White-ville." Ever seen The Stepford Wives?) As you now know my wife is brown.

Because of the strength of my paleness (i.e. pastiness), our daughter looked really white (at the time), except for her hair.

We are still buying black hair care products for my daughter. I love to go to the Sally Beauty Supply (aka black beauty supply store, to all you white people) and put a bunch of black hair care products on the counter. The cashier always looks at me like I am lost.

I'm sure she is thinking, "Does he know these are not for him?" But she is too polite to say that. Usually, it is just awkward banter until I say, "These are for my daughter."

And then we are like long lost friends. "Oh, you like sisters?" If I had known that some women of color like to hear that, I would have used that line long before meeting my wife.

Anyway. We were living in San Ramon and my wife would take the kids out to the park.

One day she came home really upset.

Me: What happened?

Her: Two ladies asked me how much I charge to nanny.

Me: What?

Her: They thought I was the nanny for my child and asked me how much I charge.

(Pause)

Me: So how much did you tell them?

Now, to me, very funny. To her, not funny.

The lesson learned? Don't always say what you are thinking.

This is also advice I would give to a younger me: Try to consider your wife's feelings in all this. It won't be easy. Sometimes, they set you up with great lines that you just want to crush, but you can't. With autism, as with life, she may be slightly more sensitive than you. I love turning everything into a joke. Just be aware that your wife may not want to hear all those jokes.

Save some for your friends.

We joke about everything, including race, in our house. There are some things you can't change.

I was sick for a week this year, and was not able to train or leave the house, making me homebound for several days with my family. When I spend an extended amount of time with my son, the reality of his condition is plainly obvious. My son's condition is severe. I love him deeply, but his condition is a constant source of stress and frustration for me.

I have anger with how things are. I struggle to understand how a friend of mine, who was a drug addict, went on to have half a dozen healthy kids by a number of different women. Another friend of mine used steroids and went on to have healthy children. I didn't smoke or drink before having kids, and my son has ridden the short bus now for 11 years.

I try to channel my anger into productive things. When I am angry, drinking does not help. Being angry and then drinking, for me, is a recipe for ending up on the show Cops. "I don't need a shirt, I'm just on my porch having a drink… officer."

Stand up comedy helps. Exercise helps. Traveling helps.

My wife says I am in a better mood when I exercise. In fact I get almost pushed out the front door most days. "Please come back after you're less angry."

69

Not sure what that says about me, but I don't think most great men had to be expelled from their own homes to burn off steam.

Mrs. Churchhill: "Winston you're just so angry. I want you out of the house. End a war or something until you calm down."

The advice I would give to a younger me would be, when I am angry, try to remember the Serenity Prayer:

God, grant me the serenity to accept the things I cannot change; courage, to change the things I can; and wisdom, to know the difference.

There are some things I cannot change. My son is mentally disabled.

There are some things I can change. I can control the activities I pursue, my attitude, the care my son receives, the school my kids go to, and my relationship with my daughter and wife.

The real difficulty is knowing the difference. Can I really control the school my kids go to? Yes and no and that's where the rub comes in; trying to fight to get my son the care he needs and then cutting myself slack when things don't go as planned. He is the reason we moved to NY, so he could go to a special school. And even after we moved, getting him into the school was a miracle.

But through it all, you have to play the hand you were dealt. You can't play the "What if?" game. No one wins with that. And to be honest, no one cares. "Yeah, if my son wasn't autistic…blah, blah, blah." "Yeah, if I was taller, I would be in the NBA." Yeah…but you aren't, so play the hand you were dealt.

That being said, just because it was not the hand you wanted or thought you would get does not mean it's not a good hand. Play it. It could turn out better than you think. Sometimes not getting what you want is the best thing that can happen to you. Pain and distress build character.

We all want to be the best. But despite what you see on TV, life is not a contest.

70

As a society we love to make lists and rank people: the most interesting people, the funniest man, the sexiest woman. Do you realize how ridiculous it is to rank people on something as subjective as interest, humor, or looks?

By definition, different people, would rank, others…differently.

We like to label things and people; where the labels we put on them determine their value. We are good at that as a society. We like to assign a numeric value to things. Things cannot just be allowed to exist but have to be ranked.

I think we are obsessed with lists because it allows us to make snap judgments and not really think about things.

No need to try new things. Someone's already made a list, and it must be true, it's on the Internet (FYI, I just heard from a banker in Nigeria. Apparently, I came into some money, so this will be my last book.)

Comparing one's self to others in pointless. You need to compare yourself to your previous self. Not to see if you're "successful", but to see if you are advancing. Are you growing? Are you maturing? Or are you regressing?

I try to do the same with my son. I try not to compare him to other 14 year olds who are playing sports or building tree houses, but to where he was 6 months ago. Is he advancing? Yes. Is he ready for Summer Math Camp? No. Has he learned to ride a bike, started to say a few words, and not destroyed a computer in 6 months? Yes on all three.

You don't have to be on anyone's top ten list to live a happy, full life.

You are you. Be the best version of you, you can be. No one can do you better than you.

NO NEGATIVE PEOPLE

I have an unusual look. I have really sleepy eyes. What were once, sometimes called bedroom eyes. They are no longer called bedroom eyes. What it means now is that, everywhere I go, people come up to me, look over their shoulder, and ask, "Hey…you got any weed?"

And if I say no, I get the look. The "seriously man, we both know you're stoned" look. Then they ask, "Well, do you have any rolling papers?" Which is seriously messed up. It's really rude.

I wouldn't go up to a heavy person, look over my shoulder and say, "Hey, you got any cupcakes?" And if they say no, I certainly don't follow up with the question, "You got any cupcake *wrappers*?"

I have had more that one doctor start an examination with, "Are you high right now? Are you sure?"

When stopped randomly by police at DWI checkpoints, I open with, "No, I have not been drinking. This is how I always look." And then I proceed to exhale forcefully into the police officer's face. Usually, the run of the mill taco breath is enough to get me on my way.

Like Bill Cosby said, "I tell you that story to tell you this story."

When I was living in the UK, I worked for the vendor management area of our office. Our area was Europe, Africa, and the Middle East. We would travel to different countries, visit companies, conduct training, and evaluate suppliers. My boss wanted to travel to France, Italy, Germany; meaning I would travel to the more "off the beaten track" countries; which suited me just fine. Who wants to go to Paris when you can go to Istanbul? Who wants to go Rome when you can go to Warsaw? Oh wait…

That being said, Istanbul is amazing. East meets west indeed. It is a spot where two religions that originated a few miles from each other meet again.

When my company sent me to Turkey, it was only for a few days. After some quick meetings I set out to explore the city. After a few short hours, it was clear I wasn't in Kansas anymore.

I wandered at a leisurely pace down İstiklal Avenue, one of the main drags in Istanbul, when I saw two kids running from the cops. The policeman --giving chase-- caught one of them and gave him a swift smack on the side of the head. Not a love pat, but a thump straight out of a Dickens' novel. I speak no Turkish, but I tried to intercede to see what was going on.

Here is what I understood from the officer: "Bad kids, steal (thump on the noggin), no good, bad, no good, childrens bad (additional thump)." I tried to tell him that maybe he should not thump children with a stick on the head, but my Turkish consists of grunts, pointing and gesticulating. I looked like a bit player from a Charlie Chaplin movie. I was trying to say, "Please don't hit him on the head anymore," by pointing, overacting, and generally making a fool of myself. The officer felt that I must not have understood.

"NO…bad childrens, steal (curling up his fingers like he was Jim Carey in *The Grinch Who Stole Christmas*) bad, (another thump on the poor kid's dirty haired noddle)." He then walked away, holding the kid by the arm, yelling at him like an angry uncle.

I considered following him, but it seemed as if my presence not only didn't help, but actually led to the kid getting extra blows to the head so this stupid tourist would understand what was happening.

Still unsure what to do in this foreign land; I wandered into a street café. It was before the dinner rush, and only one of the tables was taken. I sat down at the table next to it. Two middle-aged women were sitting at the other table. After eating, I tried to strike up a conversation with them. It was not possible. There was a lot of smiling and words, but not much was actually communicated. Our "conversation" ended up getting cut short when the bouncer came all the way from the front door to talk to me.

He was a big man. The kind of man you think of when you think of a Turkish wrestler: swarthy, hairy and no neck. Just a giant skull on two massive shoulders. His face was dominated by a mustache from another era; and a crushed nose, clearly created in this one.

He motioned for me to come with him, so I followed him to the front door. Through pointing and yelling, I determined he did not want me to talk to the two women. And more than that, he wanted me to leave. I have no idea why. Maybe one of them was his girlfriend or mother. Or maybe he just wanted to turn over the table before the dinner rush. For whatever reason, he did not like me and took to poking me in the chest when talking to me.

Now as I've said, I am not a big man (think Steve Rogers before he became Captain America, or the Disney cartoon version of Ichabod Crane, for you Boomers), but I don't like being poked in the chest. I am not tough, but being bullied as a child did one thing for me: I have little aversion to being beat up. It has happened to me before, and I am sure it will happen again.

I tried to puff my chest out and stand on my tippy toes. This only seemed to accentuate the physical difference between us. I took a good look at him…and he was big. You know you're in trouble when your plan is to punch first and run like a little girl. If it didn't go well I would probably get beat up… spend the night in jail…in Turkey…and lose my job. I dropped my head and slinked out of the restaurant. Once outside I gave a big wave and blew a kiss to the ladies and sprinted out of there.

In the words of my favorite drunk Brit: "You will never reach your destination if you stop and throw stones at every dog that barks." (Warner Kimball argued in his book that Churchill couldn't be an alcoholic as "no alcoholic could drink that much".)

After my showdown with the Turkish Ivan Drago, I was off to see the Grand Bazaar. The Grand Bazaar is something to behold (even for non-shoppers). Not everything for sale is interesting, but there are some amazing items surrounded by a bunch of made-in-China hooey.

The Bazaar is from the 1400s and the layout reflects as much. I love the chaos; but the pickpockets, not as much. Having grown up in Latin America, I am pretty cautious. My wife says paranoid. When in a large group, I cannot help but put my hand in my front pocket, the same pocket I put my wallet in. I find I am rarely pickpocketed when my hand is actually on top of the item in question. I prefer to be robbed the American way--by willingly paying too much for an item that I don't need.

In the Bazaar I bought some steel drinking glasses (for reasons I still don't fully understand) and a Kaftan coat that I have since worn on one occasion, to a costume party.

While walking through the Bazaar, I was approached by many people selling carpets.

You need to know that I have really weak sales resistance. Whenever someone is selling something, I cannot help but think of their family. "This poor guy. He probably has 7 kids to feed and needs an operation. Maybe I should buy these metal cups. Who knows? I may need cups that conduct electricity some day and they will come in handy." I buy junk I don't need, but on the issue of carpets I was firm. I was living in a tiny corporate apartment in the UK and had no room for anything.

After buying some oranges and a scarf that I didn't really want, I wandered by another carpet shop.

Carpet salesman: "Come, see carpet."

Sucker: "I don't want a carpet. Thank you."

Carpet connoisseur: "Come see, I have tea."

Target: "No. Thank you."

Carpet pusher: "Come see carpet!"

Western dope: "I don't have any room in my apartment."

Undeterred Carpet Salesman: "Come see. No buy, no problem."

Easy mark: "No thank you."

Carpetman: "Come into my shop, no pressure. We drink tea."

Weak-willed traveler: "No thank you."

So...I am in this little shop looking at carpets and the assistant is bringing out rug after rug stacked higher and higher. There is flair to it. Rugs are brought out of the back. Tea gets made, more rugs. They are thrown up in the air (the rugs, not the tea).

Carpetman: "What do think of this rug?"

Me: "It is nice, but I don't have any room for a rug where I live."

Some shouting at the assistant, more rugs, more tea. Hundreds of rugs come out of what appears to be a closet, but must have been a warehouse. I politely smile and remind him that I live in a little place in the UK. We talk a little about our families; he has grandkids that are my kid's age.

Carpet man: "What do you think about Bush?"

Weak sales resistance guy: "I don't discuss politics."

His eyes narrow, "You are a smart man." Pause. "I like you. I am going to tell you something." He looks around like people do when they are about to tell a racist joke.

"When they offer Hashish, you say 'NO Hashish.'"

"I don't smoke."

He smiles and rolls his eyes in disbelief.

"When they offer Hashish, you say 'NO Hashish.'"

"I understand. I don't smoke anything, hash or weed."

"You say you don't smoke? Ha! I can see you smoke. Listen. Turkish jail is no joke. When they offer you Hashish, say 'no Hashish.'"

After being told again by Captain Obvious how I did not want to be in a Turkish jail (who would?) I finally gave up on trying to convince him that I didn't smoke. Instead I agreed and said, "Ok, no hashish in Turkey." That made him happy. He smiled and hugged me like he just found out his new son would not be spending the rest of his life in jail. I felt a connection. There is more that unites us than divides us. Even in Turkey, people think I look like a stoner.

On my last night in Istanbul, I wanted to go out. However, witnessing yet another fistfight that afternoon, I was not sure someone like me, built with arms and legs that look like Lincoln Logs, was meant to be out after dark in Istanbul. Plus what if the rug seller was right? What if I ended up in prison and what if Turkish prisons were not fun? What if they were dreary and had no hot water? Or worse, no cable! No, this would not do. I had to come up with something. I would ask for help.

I was staying at the Crowne Plaza, on the company dime, which is great for a tightwad like me. Most of the staff were very serious--a cross between Bond villains and DMV employees.

However, there was one afternoon clerk named Hamid that was a bit of a goof ball. He was about 6'3" and easily 240 lbs. A big boy. He had a goofy smirk, and a personality that made it seem like you had known him forever.

He told these jokes when I first checked in that I am sure were hilarious in Turkish, but directly translated to English made no sense. When it was time for the punch line, he would lean across the counter, throw one of his giant meat hooks over my shoulder, and almost scream it in my face, all the while beaming.

"And then HE says, 'No! All this time you thought I was woman, but I am a man!'"

And we both laughed and laughed. About what? I have absolutely no idea. But he was having such a good time telling me; I didn't want to spoil it with a trivial thing like my comprehension.

Before I could consider whether my laughing was encouraging misogyny-ism or some other evil- ism, he was on to the next joke.

If there was anyone who could help me find a good time, while reducing the likelihood of me getting punched in the face, it was this guy.

"Hamid, hey listen, I want to go out tonight for some fun. Any ideas?"

"You want to have fun?" Hamid raises his eyebrows and shakes his "man-boobs" (what the kids call "moobs").

"Yeah, not that much fun. A little less fun than that, but more fun than this." I point to the lobby filled with what looks like to be a bunch of geriatric businessmen whispering about profit margins.

"I know THE place. It just opened. It is right on Bosporus. It's amazing—Reina."

I knew "Reina" meant Queen in Spanish, and wasn't sure whether he had the wrong idea about the kind of fun I wanted. I hoped he did not interpret my not wanting to go to a strip club as meaning I was into men, and he was now sending me to a gay bar. I tried to explain, but I was making it worse. I let it go.

"Ok, how do you get into Reina?"

"You have to be on the list."

"I am not on the list."

"I know."

"What if I pretend to be someone else?"

"Like who?"

"I don't know. Someone they would want there."

"You too ugly to be model." He says it smiling, but then nods, to make sure I know he is serious.

"Ok, yes. Didn't need to hear that, but it's true."

78

"A real celebrity, they know what he looks like."

"Yeah. Who would they not know what they look like?"

"Maybe politician. But you look like a child." Again, he was mean, but right. I was 28 at the time, but looked like I was all of 18, and that was if I wore good clothes. If I wore shorts, I looked like I might be trying out for the junior varsity basketball team.

In fact when I met suppliers for the first time, the first question was always, "How old are you?" Followed by, "Are you sure?" like I was trying to sneak into the prom.

"I know, I know, I look like a child. What if I was the son of a politician?"

His face lit up.

"Yeah, you son of famous politician…so famous we don't want to say who. We say you traveling as Mr. Smith. I like, it is good."

With that he picked up the phone and got Reina's number from someone (this was pre-Google). He gets the number and calls the club. When they answer, his voice gets deep. I mean really deep. He scowls (like I did when I heard the show Firefly was canceled). It sounds like they are talking about a nuclear agreement. The back and forth is harsh. I hear, "blah blah blah, Mr. Smith, blah blah blah," and then he hangs up the old landline with a ferocity that is no longer possible with a cell phone.

"Done". Big smile. "You're on the list as Mr. Smith. Tonight you go to Reina."

As I got ready, I was feeling nervous. When I get nervous, sometimes my mind tends to wander down a hypothetical trail where everything that can go wrong does go wrong, and always at my expense. No matter how many times I tell myself these thoughts are illogical and unlikely, I become convinced that I am somehow an Oracle and am merely foretelling my own obvious future.

The scenarios go like this. I get to Reina. They ask me who I am, I freeze, start stuttering, and finally tell them. They don't believe me. The bouncers throw me into the Bosporus, from the Bosporus Bridge. I land on a crossing oil tanker, going back to Iran. They try to figure out who I am. The bouncers yell down that I am the son of a famous diplomat. The Iranians torture me for information; I give them nothing (mostly 'cause I know nothing).

They reach out to the State Department saying that I am a spy. The State Department (rightfully) denies it, saying they have never heard of me. I spend the rest of my life in an Iranian prison making rugs to be sold in the Grand Bazaar. In Iranian prison, with no means of dental hygiene, I also lose all my teeth (this is a big deal as an American. I guess if I was from Europe, i.e. UK, no biggie).

Or how about this: I go there. I get in. I am having a good time dancing. I bump into the bouncer from the restaurant earlier that afternoon. He throws me into the Bosporus, from the Bosporus Bridge, yada yada yada, no teeth.

Or how about this: I get there. I order a coke. The bartender hands me a glass of cocaine. The rug salesmen from yesterday, accompanied by Hamid, jumps out from behind the bar and says, "Aha! I told you, no drugs!" This whole thing was a set up. I end up in prison, no teeth, etc.

The scenarios don't have to be logical, in fact, the weirder they are, the more time I have to spend convincing myself that they are not possible.

I convince myself that everyone I meet in Turkey is NOT trying to get me in an Iranian jail (so I can lose all my teeth) and I get ready.

I come down and meet Hamid at the desk.

"How do I get there?"

"There is no sign. You just need to know where you are going."

"Ok…where am I going?" Then he did what I thought was clearing his throat, but turned out to be the directions. I looked blankly at him.

"Let's get you taxi. I tell him to not rob you." Which works out great, because I prefer not to get robbed.

Hamid takes me out front to get a hotel taxi.

If you have ever taken a taxi in Turkey, you know it's a lot like a colonoscopy: rude, invasive, and not something you would think you should have to pay for.

On second thought, they are actually somewhat different. One features a lot of crying, humiliation, and leaves you sore in all the wrong places. The other is a colonoscopy.

It seems there are a limited number of taxi drivers in Turkey who are trying to provide a needed service, and there are innumerably more "taxi drivers" trying to take advantage of people who are just trying to get around.

Hamid talked to the driver. There is a lot of yelling. I would think, "Don't rob this guy, I know who you are" would be pretty clear, but there is a lot of yelling going on. The cab driver seems angry but he agrees on the price. At the time the exchange rate was over a million Turkish liras to a dollar.

"Pay him 12 million, no more!" I receive my instructions on how to make the cab driver a millionaire (with only 8 dollars), and I am off.

We pull up to a parking lot and the driver points to a door. It is an unmarked metal door with two large stones posing as men standing in front of the door. I try to ask if this is the place.

"This is it? Here?"

Freshly minted millionaire cab driver, " (Guttural sounds)."

"This is the best club in Istanbul? Reina?"

More guttural sounds.

The parking lot was full of Italian sports cars. Each car costs more than the combined value of the dozens of crappy cars I have bought over the course of my life. There is an ambulance out in front of the club and a crowd is forming.

I muster all the courage I can, exit the cab, and pay. I tip an extra 3 million Lira (2 bucks-but it sounds better in millions) in the hopes that if this is a set up, the driver will feel bad, break down, and in perfect English, tell me "don't go in there."

As I get closer, I can see the back doors of the ambulance are open and there is a man sitting inside. He is in a beautiful suit, which is covered in blood. He is holding his right hand over his right eye and blood is pouring from his face to his hand to his clothes. The suit is ruined. No one seems particularly alarmed as to the fact that someone tried to rearrange his face. He is pointing to the door of the club and yelling.

One of the bouncers standing at the door, arms crossed, raises an eyebrow a little as if to say, "I am listening but not moving. Keep talking."

The scenarios start in my head. Is this how I end up with no teeth? Maybe instead of the Iranian prison, they just punch me in the face until the teeth fall out.

I figure it is now or never. I approach the "nicer" looking bouncer, who looks like he has only killed half the number of people the psychotic one on the right has.

"Hi, fellas. My name is Mr. Smith. I'd like to come in. I think I am on the list." The only thing I could have done to make myself seem more out of place would have been to add the word "see" to the end of each of those sentences. I realize that sometimes when I get nervous my voice gets really high pitched and I start to sound like I am from the 20s. "I'd like to come in, see. I think I'm on the list, see".

The "nice" guy quickly lifted his left arm to speak into his sleeve, and I think I may have involuntary flinched. Angry words are said into his sleeve, followed by a mispronunciation of Smith.

"Wait."

This is where they have me wait until the Iranian container ship is ready to go under the bridge. They can't throw me over until the time is right.

My thoughts are interrupted by the sound of the door opening. A small woman the size of angry bouncer's thigh appears right between the two bears guarding the door.

"Mr. Smith" she says as she starts swatting their arms to make them move out from in front of the door. They both smile tiny smiles at her. Smiles, which based on their expression, look like they hurt to perform. She is small, pretty, and holding a notebook and walky-talky.

I nod and smile too, hoping this is not the part where she tells them to throw me in the Bosporus.

Lady the size of angry bouncer's thigh: "We have been expecting you." And with that I am in.

I turn sideways to squeeze by the bouncers, who still don't look like they want me in. I hurry past them, rushing in like a fool where angels fear to tread.

The tiny woman tells me, "Let me introduce you around." I meet the rich, then the famous, then the rich and famous, and then the infamous. Each group stranger than the last.

I am not sure exactly how Hamid did it, but he got me in.

People like Hamid are what make this world go round. Positive, can do people. They fuel your life, just like negative people drain your life.

That is something else I would tell a younger me:

Be positive and steer clear of negative people. One of my friends is really negative. There is a word for people like him, but my grandpa is an 80 year-old preacher who does not like four letter words. The best PG translation is: poop–stirrer.

He can take any situation, good or bad, and make sure it takes a turn for the worse. Don't think it can get worse? Wrong, he can make it worse.

He could break up the Osmonds. What? The Osmonds are broken up? You can thank him for that.

I thought I would introduce him to another negative person. My thought process was that in math a negative times a negative is a positive; not in real life it's just two really angry negative people. And they don't like to be around themselves either. Their conversation went like this:

Negative 1: "This sucks."

Negative 2: "I know. That's what I have been saying."

Negative 1: "Yeah, but I said it first."

Oh boy. Guys, you are going to have to triangulate some joy or I am going to have to subtract myself from this equation, 'cause this is not rational. I'm not wasting my half-life on you two non-zeros.

Negative people can strip you of your ability to see anything positive around you. You could be swimming in a pool of money like Scrooge McDuck and a negative person would tell you that while swimming you might tear your rotator cuff, or that the dirty money is going to give you pinkeye.

You could win the lottery and they would tell you, "The government takes half, and you know 75% of lottery winners are broke within 5 years, blah blah blah". Ok, Ok, I get it. Everything sucks and then we die. Please go tell someone else. We're all stocked up on cranky here.

Life will grind you down enough as it is. Autism can be a tough deal. My mind can get polluted with negative thoughts.

There is no need to entertain those thoughts or people. Those thoughts won't help you. Don't allow them to dissuade you from your dreams and hopes. Let those people find each other and grind each other down.

Birds of a feather flock together, and negative ones all drown each other. Steer clear and live your life with wild abandon.

REAP WHAT YOU SOW

In 1996, I graduated from college and got married in the span of a few weeks.

As school wrapped up we talked about what lay ahead for us. A lady came by our school and talked about an orphanage she started in Romania. It was the 90s, and there were a lot of street kids in Bucharest.

In the late 80's, the Romanian president was a dictator named Nicolai Ceausescu who had a policy of encouraging women to have large families. He did it through a series of draconian taxes. When the economy collapsed and people were starving, some families put their kids out on the street. It was a terrible situation. The long and short of it was there were thousands of homeless kids who, in the winters, lived in the sewers.

The lady said they were looking for help. Sounded good. We decided to go. Four weeks after our wedding, we had sold or given away everything we owned, and moved to Bucharest.

Bucharest was not exactly what we expected.

At the orphanage, I handled the accounting and payroll, among other things. At the time, the largest bill in the Romanian currency was 3 dollars. Monthly payroll was a few thousand dollars, which meant I needed to go to the moneychanger with two empty briefcases, and walk out with two full briefcases and a giant target on my back.

The most honest moneychanger seemed to be an African named Isam. He had one big gap in his front teeth, and two pistols in his belt. When I would go to see him, all he wanted to do was drink tea and talk about American culture.

"Did you ever see Michael Jordan play live?" asked Isam, sticking out his tongue.

Me: "Once."

Money dealer: "Why once? Don't like basketball?"

Me, trying to count 2000 dollars in small bills: "No, I love basketball."

Man with two guns: "Why then? See only one time?"

Me, losing my count: "I don't know. Just busy, I guess."

"You meet Arnold Schwarzenegger?"

"Uhh…no."

"Why not?"

"To be honest, I don't even know where he lives."

"Have you looked?"

"Uhh…no…"

"But you live in California? Hollywood?"

"Not Hollywood…but yeah, California."

"And you never see Rambo either?"

To Isam, "California" was just another name for "Hollywood", which was a city comprised of famous people.

In Isam's mind, there were about 200 famous people living in California/Hollywood, who would move in or out depending on their level of international popularity. If you wanted to see them, you just moved there, because of course, you could, and THEY would want YOU as a neighbor. It would be 200 famous people…plus you. I don't think he ever quite understood that I may have lived in California (but not Hollywood), but never met any of the A-list Stars he watched speak dubbed Romanian on his television.

In Romania, I started having problems with my jaw. Long story short, my top two wisdom teeth had to come out.

Dental care in Romania, circa 1996, was not world class, and I had no insurance. We ended up finding someone who knew how to pull teeth and I set up an appointment. I rode the subway to the "dentist office" which seemed more residential--y than office--y. In the lobby (read living room), I "read" an old Russian magazine. That publication should have been my first clue that this would be a truly foreign journey.

The dentist was a lady in her mid thirties with short black hair and a stare that could unnerve a murderer. She was short, pear-shaped, with a bow legged walk that said she meant business and must have ridden there on a horse. She asked that I pay the $50 in advance. Ok, no problem. I understand. I look like someone who "dines and dashes", so what's to stop me from a "pull and dash". I paid and sat in the chair, and she pulled out a Tupperware tub full of supposedly semi-hygienic instruments.

She did not speak English. We had only been in Romania a few months, and my Romanian was not great.

When she started sticking her fingers in my mouth, I gathered that I should open my mouth. After wiping a small mirror on her shirt (not joking), she tried to get it into my mouth for a look. The reason I was there was because I could not open my mouth all the way, because of the pain. I tried to explain that.

Me: "Mouth, ouch. Pain, when this (open)."

I don't believe she understood my caveman/Tonto English, so my mouth got pried open, with her assistant helping.

The assistant was even smaller than the dentist, and had a wandering eye allowing her to look at both the "dentist" and me at the same time, though I am not convinced there was much going on behind the eyes.

After my jaw had been successfully pried open, there were a series of discussions in Romanian. The part I understood was basically a number of different words all meaning "bad". Thankfully, I got two shots next. Then an instrument from the Tub came out. It hurt a lot. I made a sound that is what, I assume, a yak being castrated sounds like. I got two more shots. I felt better. New dirty instrument emerged. More pain, and this time I sounded more like a yak getting a wedgie. Two more shots. Oh yeah, much better. After 25 minutes of cutting and pulling, no actual teeth had been pulled. But I couldn't feel a thing. Other than choking on my own blood once in a while, I was fine. The dentist was telling me something that I could not have understood six shots ago, so now I have no idea what she is going on about.

Then out came a pair of needle nose pliers that looked like they were from the Russian Home Depot, circa 1940. More grunting and angling. Finally, she gets to actually removing my upper wisdom teeth. I am positioned so my head is leaning over the back of the headrest, my head almost upside down (which did not help the bleeding). One tooth came out! Yahoo. One to go.

Apparently the first tooth was easier, because the next one took even longer. They tried every position imaginable. At one point, the dentist was sitting on my lap almost straddling me with her forearm against my chest to get a better angle. The assistant was also holding my shoulders down, in case I suddenly learned how to levitate and floated away. It felt like they were pulling my spine out through my mouth. The tooth breaks. Half comes out. After more shots (caused by additional yak noises), they get the rest. (Or I thought they did. A small piece came out about a month later.)

This is the closest I have come to being drugged and abused by two women.

They sat me up, kind of smiled, wiped most of the blood off, and led me out the door.

That last part is kind of hazy.

The next thing I remember is being on the subway. Why would I take a cab? I am a man of the people…and cheap. I ride the subway. While on the subway, people are really staring at me.

In 1996, people really wanted out of Romania. You may not believe this, but in Romania I would have several women a week hit on me, often in front of my wife. (Its true. Ask her.) I am regular looking, but if girls thought you had a foreign passport and you could get them to the west, you would get a ridiculous amount of attention.

(A friend of mine, who had previously been an assistant manager at a Subway sandwich shop in the states, moved to Romania, where he had 6-foot models hitting on him almost daily. I imagine the conversation went like this, "I'm an American. And I'm an assistant manager at a subway shop. I get to make the schedule. What is your name?" "You had me at American.")

It did not occur to me that people could be staring at me, not because they wanted me, but because I looked I like was strung out, drooling, and muttering gibberish.

I got off at my stop and started slowly stumbling towards my apartment.

I told you all of that to tell you this.

At night, I worked with a feeding program, giving food to street kids. These kids where homeless, hungry, and desperate, so they often stole.

Outside my apartment building, there was a group of four young men in their early 20's, making fun of this kid who was maybe 13. And they weren't just attacking him verbally. One of them hit him on the head, another kicked him, and then they made him pull down his pants and dance.

I knew this kid. He came to the feeding program. This scene made me really mad.

As I've mentioned before, I am not a tough guy. I have what people must see as a very punchable face, based on how often they try to punch it. No one is scared of me. When people see me, they don't think, "Boy, he looks tough." They think, "Boy, that face looks super punchable."

Before I knew what was happening, I jumped in and pushed the guy who hit the kid. Then, as I started yelling, something flew out of my mouth.

As best I understood, they caught him stealing something. Another guy pushed me on the hood of a car. Now I am fluent in Spanish. Spanish is a Romance language, as is Romanian. They share some words; however, they are not the same language. After I was pushed, I went ballistic in Spanish. I pushed one of the guys, threatened their mother, told them I was going to find them in their beds while they slept, and started quoting Cypress Hill.

Another guy got in my face and there was some more pushing as we yelled at each other. Something else flew out of my mouth and hit him in the chest. More pushing, something else flew out. It took me a second to realize what it was: pieces of bloody cotton gauze. They were all over the street. It was pretty gross.

Apparently, none of them wanted to get some kind of new "Super AIDS" from a Spanish albino who could not stop bleeding from his mouth, so they started backing up.

The kid took off running. Someone said something else in a tough voice; I quoted all the NWA I could at the top of my lungs. There were some more punches thrown. I totally lost it. Red faced, crying, beating my chest, screaming 'till I was hoarse. They left.

When I got home, my wife took one look at me and said, "What happened?" I looked in the mirror. There was blood from my mouth running all the way down my chest. My shirt was soaked. My cheeks were so swollen I looked like I was storing nuts for the winter. My eyes were as blood shot as a stoner's. I looked like the walking dead.

Then I remembered having told my assailants, as best I could through pointing and waving, the building I lived in, which was just a block from the confrontation. And that I was there every day. And that they could come find me, day or night. Thankfully I don't think they spoke Spanish, especially diluted with gauze and blood.

And the best part was, I was there to work for a charity. To try to do something positive, not pick fights with random strangers while under the affects of powerful anesthetics.

Oh, and I had to go back to Dentist Ratchet (and pliers) to have the stitches put back in.

Besides having teeth pulled, living in Romania and serving in that orphanage was fun. There is joy when you do something for others that is not easy to replicate.

However, the reality is, most times, doing the right thing is not something that is always rewarded on this earth. That is something I wish I could impart to a younger me. Raising an autistic child will not be easy. If I could, I would tell myself the following about life:

There will be no parade.

There are no medals.

There will be no fanfare.

There is no award for father of the year.

There is a single father, Doug, who has twin autistic sons who attend my son's school. He is a first generation immigrant from Africa, working some menial job. He is doing his best to balance his work and crazy life.

How the Kardashian girls make millions of dollars doing nothing, I am not sure. But that is not something Doug can do.

There will be no line of perfume called Doug the Cab Driver's *Desire*.

No reality show of his life.

No cabbie line of clothes, with matching accessories.

No one wants to be him, and no one wants to be you.

Cleaning up messes. Bathing, dressing and wiping the bum of a disabled person the rest of his life. No one wants a piece of that.

Caring for a mentally disabled person will not make you famous. No one is giving out gift bags to the teachers who work at my son's school. Restaurants don't clamor when they stop in. They will not be included in any list of the most beautiful or interesting.

This will not make you famous.

This line of work offers no swag, few accolades and no awards. However don't let that dissuade you from pursuing it.

There may not be five nationally televised award shows like actors have (boy, actors really don't get the recognition they deserve), but that does not make it less valuable or important.

Not everything in life can be measured with decimal places, awards, or mouse clicks. Don't look to others to show you what you know in your heart to be important. Don't look for adulation for doing the right thing. The right thing is done for its own reasons. Don't look for a stranger to confirm what has been written on your soul. It is there and you know it.

Don't be disheartened, sow good things. In time there will be rewards, though not necessarily the kind you are looking for.

Don't worry; you will reap what you sow.

NO FEAR

I have had the opportunity to travel to Turkey a few times. I call Turkey the land of the non-ironic mustache. Brooklyn, eat your heart out.

It seems everyone there has a mustache, including the men. Zing. This is a place where the men are men and the women are…manlier than me.

Seriously, it is a beautiful country. The people are very friendly. Strangers paid for my tea four different times and once for a meal. I felt like the belle of the ball.

I was excited when I got the chance to go back to Turkey, and hoped it would be as fun as the first time I went. It did not disappoint. Here is the travel log:

Day One

Up at my usual wake up hour: 5 am (this is where everyone who knows me laughs). Really, I am up because of the jet lag. I take the tram down to the Blue Mosque. The 6 am tram is packed. I find out it is because today is a holiday. It is called Kurban Bayrami. It is a festival celebrating Abraham sacrificing a ram instead of his son.

I follow the crowd and end up going into the Blue Mosque. It's morning prayers on a religious holiday, so it is standing room only. I pray (to my God) and take a few pictures as discretely as possible and exit. No international incident. At the exit, they are giving out this lentil sorba (soup). It was delicious.

On to the Hagia Sofia. There is some sort of protest blocking the entrance. There are over 50 policemen in full riot gear, including shields. People have signs and are protesting something. There is anger. I decided to not press my luck and I move on.

Down to the Bosporus. I take a ferry ride over to the Asian side of Istanbul. The ride is amazing. Perhaps the best $1.50 I have ever spent, and I am cheap. I have a late breakfast at Filizter. The restaurant offers an incredible view of Leander Island.

I take a different ferry ride to the northern (European) side of Istanbul. I walk down to the Bosporus Bridge and walk by Reina. It is almost unrecognizable in the daytime (especially sans the mountainous bouncers).

I have a Donner and a salty yogurt drink…the drink is not my favorite.

From there I walk to Taksim. I get lost. An uneventful 5 km walk takes me three hours…'cause I am an idiot. The main drag off Taksim is one of my favorite streets in Istanbul. So cool. From there to the Galata Tower. The line is long (and I have been before), so I decide to not go in. From there, I go to the Galata Bridge, then tram it back to the place I'm staying.

I meet my host, Basma, who has made baklava. I share some with other tourist guests and then I crash. I calculate that I walked about 7 miles. That, plus the jet-lag, is killing me. For the first time in a long time, I go to bed before 7pm.

Day Two

I have come to terms with the fact that everyone here has better facial hair than me.

Not being able to sleep meant I was out on the street at 5:30 am, even before UPS. A restaurateur at the end of the street where I am staying was sure I was going to be robbed and insisted I stay in the restaurant until the trams started running. I did, and had 2 bowls of lentil soup, and talked to a few people there. A customer paid for the soup, because, "America, is like, this the time, AMERICA." I have no idea either. That is what he said, verbatim. The soup was delicious.

Next it was down to the Blue Mosque area, then on to the Yeni Galata Bridge to get a good view of the sunrise. I grow impatient and decide to move farther east to get a better view.

I walk along the road leading east, which is called, drum roll please, Kennedy Avenue. Not sure why the coastal road in the old part of Istanbul is named after the Irish, but there you have it.

The sunrise is awesome.

There is a sign on the rocks on the water's edge saying, "No Swimming". Next to the sign, there is a group of 20 old men, swimming, covered in hair and little else; doing belly flops, flabby arms slapping at the water. They try to convince me to come in the water. I pretend I don't understand. Not sure if it is the water's filth or the temperature, but the whole thing doesn't sound very tempting.

I walk along the water's edge. There are literally dozens of cats. I'm guessing they're playing a game of literal "cat and mouse", or, perhaps, "cat and rat".

Arrive at the Little Hagia Sophia, I don't see the resemblance to the actual Hagia Sophia. The actual Hagia Sophia is overwhelming. A building that has dominated the skyline and the city from even before it was called Istanbul. This Little Hagia Sophia is nothing like it. It's small and pedantic.

I try to head to the Blue Mosque and Hagia Sophia again (which are next to each other), but I get lost. When I get to the Hagia Sofia, the line is long, so I do not go inside.

I go to the Grand Bazar.

The restaurateur from the morning had recommended a Turkish bath, which involves a mustached man beating you. Sounds like the Turkish massage originated in the Turkish prison. I decided I wanted to try it.

I try to find the Hamam (Turkish bath), but, surprise, I get lost. I get a cup of coffee.

At this point, I realize I have had two bowls of lentil soup and a coffee. I need to find a bathroom, stat. While convinced I am going to have to deal with a Turkish toilet (which is just a hole in the ground), I fortunately do not. It is a regular toilet, except there is no toilet paper. I talk to the female attendant who, at first, wants to give me a piece of notebook paper; a painful proposition. Eventually I get toilet paper. Disaster averted.

Day Three

I have looked for a local Hamam (Turkish bath) for several hours.

I finally find one. I am the only customer. Never a good sign, but it is still a holiday here. However, being the only customer, I am sure I'm going to be kidnapped and held for a ransom befitting my social status, (I'm guessing, roughly 18 dollars). And I'm confident that Liam Neeson wouldn't use his "certain set of skills" to get me back either.

All three workers have serious mustaches that would put Tom Selleck to shame.

I don't speak Turkish and no one speaks any of the languages I do speak. Through a series of gestures and grunts, I am told to get naked and put a towel on (at least that is what I think they are telling me). Then I am sent into a steam room.

I don't know how hot it was or how long I'd been there, when I start to hallucinate. The celling is domed and has several tiny little windows. Several of the windows start to look like they compose a face. Then the face winks at me. I am starting to lose it.

Before entering this little corner of hell, I was worried that the massage might be too rough, but that was before being in a room so hot it convinces your mind that the structure of the building is making a pass at you.

At that point I was ready to get out of the room with the animated celling, and if that meant going into another room to be beaten like a rented mule, so be it.

I hope that little room is as close as I ever get to a Turkish prison.

The masseuse comes to get me. After dousing me with water like a burning man, he started the cleaning. I never thought I would be cleaned by another man. At least not until my old age, when my children abandon me to a rest home.

He put on a mitt (whose official name is number 8 sandpaper), and then proceeded to lift a few unneeded layers of skin from me. As you can imagine, it is an intimate experience to be cleaned by another human.

After that comes the soap. It is not Neutrogena, or some fancy soap from Fight Club. It is industrial strength soap. The kind they used in Dickens' novels to clean chimney sweeps, and the Soviets used to use to take unnecessary layers of paint off a tank.

Once you are soaped up, they start pulling joints and kneading you like a pizza.

After being turned into a pizza, I was done. I sat there in a towel, trying to gather my strength so I could go pay them for the punishment.

After changing back into my clothes, I almost sprinted out of that gulag.

Next, I wanted to go see the Aqueducts called Valens, but....you guessed it, I got lost. I eventually found them, but not before having everyone I asked for directions give me tea.

I guess the lesson is, if in Turkey and you want some free tea, ask someone for directions.

The age of the city of Istanbul is hard to comprehend. The Blue Mosque was a mosque for over 400 years, but before that it was a church for over 1400. The age of the city is astounding. It makes the UK, which us Americans consider old, look like a toddler.

Some of the history of the city would be hard to believe if it were not for some historical remains confirming the fact.

While touring the Basilica Cistern the guide said, "There used to be a huge church here. Don't believe me? You can still see the Basilica cistern; a cistern bigger than a football field, that has stood the test of time."

It is amazing that they built a cistern that lasted over 1500 years. We don't build stuff like that any more. Does my generation build things like that? My iPhone only lasts 2 years. And that is if I don't let water, the most ubiquitous resource on the planet, touch it.

Day Four

Women never try this with me.

There is no good place to start this story, so I'll start at the beginning. I had been eating breakfast at the same place the last few days. The restaurateur, who was the one who recommended the Hamam, had been really nice and helpful.

So I return to his restaurant and again have the lentil soup. Delicious. It is 6 am when I get there. The owner is very friendly. He tells me about his four children and girlfriend. I tell him about my wife and kids.

He invites me to come to his house for tea when he gets off work at 9 am. I am going to do several hours of sight seeing and say I'll stop by afterwards.

The Turkish are noted for their hospitality. I have had more than a handful of strangers buy me tea over the last few days, so I think nothing of the offer. I am not sleeping well because of the jet lag, so I have been up since 4 am. Stopping to sit on someone's couch sounds nice.

Now, looking back, there are signs that not all is as it seems. They seem obvious in hindsight, but at the time, I chalk them up to cultural misunderstandings.

I get lost but eventually find his place.

The first obvious sign that something was awry was that he answered the door in shorts...that were rolled up, giving himself a wedgie like a sumo wrestler. I tried to ask what's the deal with the Nacho Libre ensemble, but something is lost in translation.

Oh, and he tried to give me a kiss on the mouth. I was so distracted by the wedgie attire, I barley turned my head in time to make sure the kiss was on the cheek. My mind raced as I tried to remember if I had seen men kiss each other on the mouth here. I remember the head bumping and cheek to cheek touching...maybe I missed the kissing somehow.

He offers me a seat on the couch. I sit down. Then he offers me some wine. It is 10 am. "No, thank you."

"Are you sure?" Uhh, yeah, I am sure I don't want to drink any wine…at 10 am…in Turkey…in a house with a strange man wearing a thong.

"Are you tired? Do you want to lie down?" Uhh, again, no. Not interested in lying down while you dance around in a speedo.

Then the gifts come out. Why gifts, you ask? I have no idea. Gifts for my kids. Gifts for my wife. So he definitely knows I am married. Am I being courted?

"Sorry. I can't take your gifts. I have to go."

He tells me his children never call. He says that one should think only of one's self. Uhh, ok. But maybe you should think of yourself before you roll your shorts up so high that you cut off circulation.

He says he does whatever his heart tells him. If his heart tells him to sleep with a woman, he does. If his heart tells him to sleep with a man, he does.

"Excuse me?"

Ok, there you go. I am not interested in sleeping with men. My heart, body, and soul are in complete agreement on that one.

"Sorry, I really have to go."

"Are you CIA?" What? No. But if I was, I would not tell you. Who would say yes to that question? Only people not in the CIA. CIA guys would say no. Most non-CIA guys would say no. Plus, who can tell a man with a wedgie, "Yeah, I'm a spy," and keep a straight face.

Maybe it was some sort of weird internal justification on his part. I was rebuffed. The guy must be CIA. The only straight men who can stand up to the sensual charms of a 60 year old man with a wedgie and wine teeth at 10 am are Spooks.

That's the problem? That I am CIA? Not that you're trying to get a conscious, heterosexual man to have sex with you when you have purple wine teeth, are 20 years older than me and…oh yeah, I'm not gay? Darn those CIA agents and their training.

Me: "I have to go."

Wedgie man: "Maybe I'll come see you in New York."

Me: "Uhh, ok. Maybe email me some time. What? You don't do email?"

Wedgie man: "How will I find you?"

Uhh, I don't know. But I am not giving my physical address to a little man-who's coming on to me, and who thinks: confused stranger, plus 10 am, plus wine, plus wedgies equals party.

Wedgie man: "I will find you."

Uhh, Ok. Not so sure you will. You weren't even able to find pants. "I have to go."

"Take the gifts."

"I can't take the gifts."

"Take the gifts."

"I can't take the gifts."

"TAKE the gifts."

"Ok, I am taking the gifts," because I am not going to stand around arguing the rest of the morning with a man in his underwear.

I checked around for cameras to make sure I was not on candid camera, thanked my host for one of the weirdest mornings of my life, and bolted.

Not exactly Turkish delight.

This is one of the craziest stories that happened to me last year and it happened cause I took a chance. That is something I would tell a younger me, take chances.

Sure it won't always work. Sometimes they will lead to something embarrassing, unfunny or slightly scary but you have to try things. You can't live your life in fear. You cannot avoid pain and death by running from life. This reminds me of the story *Death Came to Baghdad*. It is believed to be a ninth century Middle Eastern teaching, by Fudail ibn Ayad from Hikayat-i-Naqshia (although it probably dates to before that).

The basic story is a man goes to the market in Baghdad and bumps into the physical incarnation of death. Death gives him a weird look, scaring the man. The man then borrows a horse from his boss to escape to Damascus as he is sure Death has it in for him. After the man flees to Damascus his boss goes to the market to confront Death. He asks Death, "Why did you scare my worker?" To which Death says, "I was not trying to scare him, I was just surprised to see him here. I have an appointment with him tonight, in Damascus."

Everyone has a time and an hour. Don't over think it. Do your best. Try your hardest. Take chances. Live your life.

CONTRIBUTE

I met with a social worker recently. I was trying to navigate the system to get my son into an after school program. I thought it would be good for him to get some exercise and stay active after school instead of zoning out in front of the tube everyday. There are after school programs designed for him. In fact, there is one at his school. One cannot pay for it out of pocket, or through insurance (neither of which are realistic options anyway), it can only be covered by the state. No problem, you say, your kid is diagnosed as autistic and cognitively delayed (the new term for the old term of retarded); you should have no problem getting coverage. That is when the flying monkeys come in.

We moved to NY several years ago to get him into this and other programs like it. We started the application process for the program as soon as we arrived. My wife has filled out hundreds of forms. (I knew that college degree would come in handy.) First we had to prove that he had a disability, which is crazy. A two-minute visit with any doctor always ends with, "Your son is seriously disabled." Uh yeah, I know, that is why we are here, sweet cheeks.

So after hundreds of dollars of out of pocket costs to prove something that random strangers are telling us at the grocery store, we have the paperwork to prove something as obvious as the nose on your face.

Then you navigate the very interesting people who work in this endless maze of bureaucracy. There are four kinds of people working in this field.

1. People who really don't want to help you and even if they could they would not. In fact you being on fire does not mean they will stop to spit on you.
2. Then there are the people who want to help but don't know what they are doing. So you waste MONTHS until you figure out it is the "blind leading the blind" and get frustrated. (It takes months to figure out they never filed the right papers and

that's the reason your application is stuck, and they are stalling.)

3. Then there are those who might be able to help you if they wanted to but are:
   a. Too burnt out to help
   b. Have personal problems they are trying fix while working
   c. Don't care
   d. Are playing games on their phones
   e. All of the above

4. Then there are the blessed few. People who know how to do their jobs, want to help you, and got into this field to help people. People who are trying to help out their fellow humans are very rare indeed.

One of them asked me, what are my hopes for my son? It's a great question that I get asked a lot.

The answer is that they are the same as they are for my daughter who is "regular".

Let me put it another way. There is a singer whose voice puts many of the singers on the radio to shame.

But, I hear you say, "Can he write his own music?" Oh, Yeah.

"But can he play an instrument?" Instrument? No. Instruments? Yes.

"Can his music make you feel like all is right with the world, that there is hope, and that all is not lost?"

Yes, Yes and Yes.

His name is Raúl Midón. You may have seen him on the Late Show with David Letterman years ago.

Born premature, he was put into an incubator without the proper eye protection. He is now blind. At a young age, his father taught him to drum and his journey with music began. NOW, he is an incredibly gifted musician. But he was not born that way. It took someone taking the time to teach him (and him putting the time and work into developing his art). It is parenting. It is time consuming. It is work.

NOW, he contributes to society.

That is what every parent of a kid who is not "regular" hopes for. That their child will contribute. It does not have to be in a traditional way, but we hope for a contribution, that our children would find fulfillment in the experience. That it would be rewarding, stimulating and fulfilling.

That is the piece of advice I would give to a younger me. Contribute. Make a contribution to improving this little rock called Earth. Be part of the solution not the problem. Midón does not contribute to society in an easily measurable way (giving joy is difficult to measure), but he definitely contributes. Midón contributes to society in a way a thousand regular dudes do not.

His music gives me a feeling of euphoria, a belief that anything is possible. Here's to the hope that my contribution to the world would be equal to that which the "disabled" can make.

NOT ABOUT YOU

I ride a motorcycle. My son likes me to take him on rides on the back of the bike. The problem is, I have a sport bike, so he sits slightly above and behind me. And he is big. While he's not scared, he still likes to hold on very tight. Also, when he gets excited, he likes to let out these little yelps. The more excited he gets, the tighter he holds on. So as we travel he is squeezing me with all his might, yelping to his heart's content. My face is red from the squeezing and from him sitting almost on top of me. At stoplights, people give us funny looks. "Ah, isn't that sweet? That special dad is taking his special son on a special ride. Isn't that special? Don't stare they might get angry."

When my son wants something, he points at it. When he wants to ride the motorcycle, he comes out and points at the motorcycle.

We were in a parking lot once, and next to our 10 year old white Mazda there was a brand new white BMW, and he points to the BMW, as if to say, "lets take this one." I'm not sure that is autism. That is kind of just how guys talk. Have you ever been at a restaurant with a friend, and your friend is elbowing you, pointing at a girl and grunting, "Huuh"? What do you do? You raise eyebrows, smile, let out a few, "ahhs" and "ehh"s, raise your shoulders and nod your head at her, all the time still grunting.

He points at the food he wants too. He is a big fan of food, usually in unusual combinations. One is of his favorites is Rice Krispies with Ketchup. It does sound weird but tastes ok. It is not a snack you would think to try but it is not terrible. It is a metaphor for our life. Our lives are not what we imagined they would be, they are different, not terrible just very different, like Rice Krispies with Ketchup.

In addition to autism, we think my son has Tourette's syndrome. He does not yell out cusswords, probably because he does not know any, but he repeats certain phrases and sounds. At nine, his favorite was "peek", which he would pronounce in a high pitched squeal. He would also say

"Oh man" like it was a catch phrase from a 1980s sitcom. The "peek" sound is hard to describe in written form. What my wife and I called that sound, was the demented duck sound. Strange, but true. It sounded like a duck that had some problems enunciating, finally lost touch with reality and his fellow ducks, decided to go all in. Like a quack that was higher pitched, louder, and more grating than the duck from the Aflac commercials. More grating than Gilbert Godfried trying to sell Aflac? Yes. Hard to believe, but true.

I am not sure what he is thinking when launching into one of these repeated outbursts. From the outside, it looks, to me, like he is bursting to get the sound out of his body. It is as if there is a sound creator inside of him. It creates these high pitched squeals and yelps, and they have to come out. It is as if he is anxious to share with the world these little bits of knowledge, and the successful vocal exit of the sound creates great joy in him. It is clear, from the expression on his face, he hopes the joy will be shared. That his little squeal will be met by a reciprocal squeal. But alas, I don't speak squeal, and all I can do is imitate it as best I can, smile and laugh. Normally, that is enough.

This was also the time of our lives when he would line up and stack everything. He would line up anything he could get his hands on. All his VHS tapes were stacked and in line. All of his toys out on the floor were in a line that circled around the room. Each item perfectly lined up, touching the item in front and behind it, like a giant chorus line of toys ready to dance for our delectation and delight.

However, it was not a homogeneous group of toys. Any number of items could be pulled into the fray. Trucks to tanks, cars to cats, to dinosaurs both green and purple, to pilfered pans, all lined up. Each forming a part of a constant line along the floor, up the dresser, under the bed, and then looping back on itself. If you wanted something from the line, you could take it and try to replace it with an acceptable alternative. Would he find the alternate acceptable? It was hard to predict. It did not have to be the same size or weight, but he was resolute on whether it was acceptable or not. I am sure there was an algorithm in his head that made that determination, but I was not privy to that level of information.

The line of things in his room was fine. It was when it would extend to the rest of the house, and include things you might want or need, like your cellphone, keys or a piece of pizza, that it got complicated. The line might be there a few days, and you might not want your keys included in the line, right in the middle of the floor, just sitting there until he got tired of them and replaced them with a different item. Tomorrow may bring a line of mostly forks, with a few couch pillows interspersed. Who knows? Everyday was an adventure.

We would normally put all the things back when he was asleep or at school, but he would always discover our chicaneries and begin to create his art with renewed vigor. A couple of Philistines disguised as parents would not dissuade him.

He must have felt like Howard Roark with my wife and I playing the villains in his little adventure, always standing against his attempts at becoming the next big thing in the art industry. "How can I become the next Warhol under these circumstances?!?"

I wondered what was going on his mind. Does he consider us backward hillbillies who don't understand what is involved in this master craft? Is it all he can do to not shout at us for the lack of order in his house? Does he consider himself kind of like the "Autistic Eye for the Straight Guy", having to go around trying to fix our squalid little lives? Or maybe he feels he is an unappreciated feng shui master trapped in the west, and if he was born 200 years earlier (and in China), he would have been idolized.

Normally, his "straightening up" of everything and little yelps are not much of a problem. You just grin and bear it. However, on a road trip out west one Christmas, it drove me to the brink of insanity. We decided that it would be a good "adventure" to drive from Texas to California for Christmas. Driving for 12 hours, for three days, the four of us, in a compact car. One of the days, we stopped somewhere in New Mexico in the middle of the night to try to get some sleep. He had been really good that day, so you knew it could not last. Around one am, he started making the demented duck noise. "Peek, peek, peek," every 90 seconds, like clock work. I tried to ignore it the first 10 minutes, both me and my wife shushing him.

Wife: Shhhhh.
Boy: Peek.
Wife: Shhhhh, quiet.
Boy: Peek, Peeeek.
Wife: Shhhh, its time for night night.
Boy: Peek.
Wife, trying to gently get him to cover his mouth: Shhhh.
Boy: (muffled) Peek, Peek, Peek.

After 20 minutes of that, I started laughing. There was absolutely nothing we could do. The kid would not be quiet. The "peeks" started getting louder and happier. He was not peeking to be a Pecker; he was a happy little pecker, peeking the night away. There was nothing we could do to stop it. As inconvenient as it was, there are other times where it would have been worse.

I was thinking, "What if we were Jews, hiding in Anne Frank's attic, and the Nazis are walking by? We would be toast."

They would look around:
Nazi: Iz anyone here?
Boy: Peek.
Nazi: No, it's only a disturbed duck.
Boy: Oh man.
Nazi: A duck that, apparently, is bilingual and has its own catchphrase.

Or, what if we were at a wedding and the minister gets to the crucial part.
Minister: If there is any reason these two should not be joined...
Boy: Peek.
Minister: What reason does do you–
Boy: Peek.
Minister: Do you have a reason tha--
Boy: Peek, Peek.

Minister: Well I think its clear tha--
Boy: Peek, Peek, Peek.
Minister: This can't go forward until this duck is removed.
Boy: Oh man.

Younger Kirk, here is a hard lesson: It is not always going to be about you. I know, Madison Avenue is telling you otherwise but it is truly not all about you. Be flexible. Things around you that annoy you are not always being done to get under your skin. Once you get your head around the fact that everything doesn't revolve around you, you will be easier to be around and people will be drawn towards you. Ironically giving you the attention you need.

BE JOYFUL

As he gets bigger, I am concerned for him and what his future holds. When you have a son, as a man, you want that son to be big. When you find out he has neurological issues, you want good things for him, but you just want him to be smaller so you can still control him when he gets out of hand. With a regular kid, you want him to be built like a line backer. With an autistic kid, you want him to be built like a referee. A regular kid you want built like a Viking. An autistic kid you want built like an IKEA worker. Both are Swedish, but one is into pillaging and the other is into pillows.

I guess what I am saying is, you are hoping your autistic kid is built not for Ultimate Warrior but Ultimate Frisbee. My son, however, is very strong; in fact when he gets old, I am going to have to hire ultimate fighters as babysitters. My interview questions will be, do you know jujutsu? Do you know how to make a grown man wear his pants? Are you a fan of ketchup?

It's not all negative, though. There are some positives.

Positive things about autism: I don't worry about empty nest syndrome; at this rate, the nest will never be empty. Also I don't have to save for college. The biggest hurdle to him getting into college is not money; it's nudity.

I'm also not concerned about him using illegal drugs. People use drugs to disconnect from reality. He is already disconnected from reality. He is not trying to escape the pressure of life. He doesn't have any traditional pressure. He does not seem to be worried about anything; not health insurance, rent money, not even watching the new DVD of Kung-fu Panda (which is awesome by the way). Whenever he has a problem, he says, "Dada." That's it. I am his answer to everything. I am what calms him down. I am his drug. I am his autistic version of weed. I imagine a drug addict sees him and thinks, "That kid is high all the time. What's he on? Autism? Man, all the best stuff is pharmaceutical."

I guess it is true; no one is happy with what they have. People take drugs to tune out. My son is tuned out and I am doing everything I can to get him to tune in. Regular people do anything they can to get messed up, and I am trying to do everything I can to try to get my son to be regular. Basically, everyone is trying to get what they don't have. If you have straight hair, you want curly hair; if is brown you want it blond and if you are bald you just want hair.

It sounds so small, but I just want him to communicate. In the store one time, he wanted M & M's. He pointed very clearly at them. I made him say "M & M's." He said it and then said his version of "thank you". He has a hard time pronouncing the "th" sound, so it sounds an awful lot like he is saying f*** you, but I was happy to hear it. The lady in line behind me probably thought I was a little unbalanced when I congratulated him on telling me to "f-you", but that's where he is. At this point, he could tell me, "Dad, you're jackass, and I hate you!" And I would reply, "Good job son. Good talking. Have I ever told you how proud I am of you? Now tell me again how you think I'm a moron, a doofus, a dimwit, and this time use your whole vocabulary. Oh, you know what I would like for Father's Day? I'd like you to write me a 10 page paper on why I'm a ding dong. And be articulate. Use the big words."

They say having kids humbles you, and it does. But having an autistic kid really humbles you. I can tell you, wiping someone else's butt for a decade will really humble you. You ever have a good day at work, then come home to wipe the bum of someone who is almost your same size? He can't even say "Please." He just points. I mean who runs this asylum; the man wiping or the man being wiped?

I sometimes feel like he is my prison cellmate, and he owns me. Do you know how gangster it is to make eye contact with someone, then just take a poop? The subtext is, "Yeah, I just pooped. And you're going to wipe my bottom and there is nothing you can do about it."

One of the more difficult things about my family's situation is thinking about the future. Thinking about taking care of your child for your whole life is beyond overwhelming. This kid could live with me the rest of his life. That is long-term commitment, and it is a little scary. I don't even have a cell phone contract. I am month to month with my cell phone company. Raising an autistic kid can last forever. Even marriage isn't forever anymore. But you can't get an annulment from a handicapped child. "Listen Johnny, this just isn't working out. Let's get the priest to say a few words, get this relationship annulled, and we can both move on. When we got together, we were both so young and dumb. It was a crazy weekend in Vegas. Let's just say what happened in Vegas stays in Vegas."

My son does not always understand what I am asking him to do. How do you get someone to do something when they don't understand what you want from them? Often we have to make him do stuff, by doing what is called hand over hand, where you put your hand on top of his hand and make him do something. Which is fine for now. He is currently big, but it is still possible to make him do something. He is soon going to be bigger, stronger but still younger than me, and I am afraid he is going to kick my butt. Like one day he'll wake up and realize, "Wait a minute. I am bigger than you Dad, and the answer is no". He'll just put me in a headlock, start dragging me around, spanking me. "This is for making me brush my teeth."

A regular kid you can negotiate with. You tell him, "Listen, if you don't do what I say, I will take this video game away from you." If I tell my son that I will take something away from him, he just stares at me blankly as if I am talking about Quantum mechanics. "Yeah son, this is the description of physical systems via a mathematical structure, it's called the wave function." And he's looking at me like, "I want cookies." You can't threaten to take away a phone or video game that he does not know how to use.

And he is sweet, but he has a look that can be a little intimidating. I don't look intimidating. I always wanted to look like a man's man, but I look more like another man's man. I wanted to look like a man that other men are scared of, not attracted to. Some guys you see and you think, "Look at that guy. He looks like if you punch him you'll just make him angry." People see me and think, "Look at that guy. He looks like if you punch him you'll make him cry and then he'll tell his boyfriend on you."

I am going to have to start P90X just to make this kid get in the bathtub. He is bulky. He has been working out since he was 2 to the Wiggles. He's busier than a one-armed paperhanger. Between protecting myself from him and protecting my daughter from perverts, I feel like I should be taking Jujitsu classes; or at least buying *Tap-out* t-shirts. (You know who you are. Fake it till you make it.)

He is just really physical. When he is angry, he head-butts. When he is happy, he head-butts. When he gets excited, he head-butts. He's like a little soccer hooligan. Once he got really excited and head-butted me so hard he gave me a big lump. And believe me, you don't know real love until you've received the Glasgow-kiss and complementary lump.

In a lot of ways, he is a regular kid. He has good days and bad days. I often wonder which JJ is going to show up today. Is it going to be the little guy who wants to hug and tickle, or the Tasmanian Devil who head-butts and destroys everything in the house. The likelihood of something being destroyed seems to have a direct correlation to how valuable it is. Let me explain. If I got it at a garage sale, it will last forever. If it is electronic and/or fragile, he wants to stomp on it and then take it to the bathtub.

He is also a wily little one. An accomplished escape artist, with no formal training, he once got naked and escaped a locked house in 6 seconds flat. He was knee high at the time and the cops picked him up. My wife found him in the cop car. He liked playing with the lights, and he wouldn't get out of the car. He could not answer the officers' questions as he does not really talk. And being that he was much lighter skinned than my wife, they did not believe that she was his mother. She had to show them a family picture that included me where I was white, naked and covered in ketchup, so they could see the family resemblance.

And it is not just escaping; he has mastered other areas of stealth. He likes to get naked and come into our room in the middle of the night like a clandestine operative. And he just stands there at the foot of the bed, like the little kid from *The Ring*. It's scary to wake up in to the middle of the night with a little naked man standing there, pointing, like the evil monkey from *Family Guy*.

He is still at the point where he just thinks everything is about him. When I take him to McDonalds, if I don't keep an eye on him, he just helps himself to people's food as we walk by. One time, I was in McDonalds and this lady was giving me the evil eye. I was trying to figure out, "Do I know this lady? Did we go to school together?" Then I looked down at her table. Right in the middle of her three kids is my son, eating all their food. Saved me 8 dollars.

He is not malicious; he just thinks it is all about him. On his sister's birthday we have to get him a present or he freaks out. He can't understand that it is not about him. She will have her friends over, and they will dance in the living room to some music. And he will be there the whole time, thinking it is about him.

I am guessing he's thinking, "This was a good day. There was cake. There was fire on the cake; I like that. You brought over some hoochie mamas to dance for me; I liked that. I tried to grab their butts and pretended I didn't understand. That was great. You two are the best parents/wingmen that anyone could ever ask for."

Having a 15-year-old daughter is different. She is smart and beautiful. She is taller than her mom and getting all the women bits. And I don't like that.

My friends don't help. Some of them are jerks. When they meet her for the first time they do that "Avoiding Prison Math", also known as "Pedophile Algebra". You can see the wheels turning in their heads. And then the question comes:

Jerk: "Ok if she is 15 now, when she is 18, I will be…"

Kirk: " A thousand feet away, you piece of garbage."

When I was younger, it never occurred to me that I could have a daughter and she could be beautiful.

We were three boys until my parents had my sister when I was 13. By that time, I was already at boarding school. So for my formative years it was just the three boys. I remember starting fires in the house, fights in our underwear (which we thought made us wrestlers), BB gun wars, and fistfights. You know, guy stuff.

When I would think of raising kids, I would think of ways to make sure that my three boys didn't kill each other...until they were on a sports field. (One of my dad's favorite pictures is my brother Henry playing catcher, trying to cover home plate, while I try to run over him.)

Those were the kinds of problems I was thinking about trying to navigate when I thought about having kids, not trying to decide if I should put the time in to learn Muay Thai or just buy a gun because of the attention my daughter was getting.

Just to give you some context, she was once asked out by a Junior when she was in 8th grade. I was not happy.

Things with a daughter are different. When I was a kid, I remember my brothers and I having to be spanked twice--once by my mom, but again by my dad when he got home--because we would not stop laughing when my mom would spank us. With my daughter, I can give her the look and say her full name, and she'll get tears in her eyes. Tears. Actual tears.

People ask what my daughter's relationship with her brother is like; it can be summed up with a quick story. My daughter is an honor student. We have only been called to the principles office once for her. It was when she was 5 and she had bloodied a little boy's nose with a straight right. I asked what happened. She said, "He called JJ stupid. I don't like people calling him stupid. He is not stupid, he is just different." Not much I could stay to that. It never happened again and the boy didn't call him stupid any more.

She is a sweet girl. I would die for that girl. That is not hyperbole. I hope some of you boys at her school are reading this. Don't underestimate a bird-boned old man with nothing to lose. I am not afraid of a few years in jail. Yeah, I have a pretty face (some would say a prison "girlfriend" face), but jail could be sweet relief: 10 hours of sleep, no emails to answer and I don't have to work. Next you're going to tell me I'd get health care and cable television. I am not kidding, mess with my little girl at your own peril, I train with a 14 year-old autistic boy who is crazy strong and has a penchant for head butting.

JJ is so physical; I think he would like sports. Of all of the dreams I had for him, the dreams of him playing college sports were the hardest to let go.

But as things stand now, the dreams I had for my son to play college sports have died. The only sport I think he might be able to do is wrestling, and that is only if they start to allow tickling (and head-butting). Maybe he could do track, but only if he did not have to run in a straight line, and he could do it in the nude like the original Olympians. (He loves to be naked. That's his thing.)

Letting go of the dreams I had for him was hard. If I could tell my younger self anything about this it would be the following:

You have dreams for him that will die.

Dreams of watching him play college sports, gone.

Dreams of watching him walk the line in high school and college, gone.

Dreams of him playing point guard for the Knicks, and you leeching off him, gone. (Tagging along on his jet, borrowing his convertible Stingray Corvette, front row seats next to Spike Lee, gone, gone and really gone.)

Kübler-Ross said there are 5 stages of grief: Denial, Anger, Bargaining, Depression and Acceptance.

That is not how it was for me.

For me it was more like:

Denial

Anger

Bargaining

More Anger

Depression

Little bit of Anger

Acceptance

Have your heard of Anger?

Then back to the beginning.

That is why I like to box.

Younger Kirk, there are some things about your future that you need to know:

Everything in your life has just changed.

You may not feel the magnitude of how it has changed, but oh, it has changed. Remember how just having a regular kid changed everything? Well having an autistic kid has changed it again.

The life you thought you were going to have is gone. That is not all bad. Life is unpredictable, and not having an autistic kid is no guarantee that your life would turn out as planned anyway, but now it definitely won't turn out as planned.

You can be a little sad about this if you want, but don't fight it. It won't work. I am telling you from experience. Get your head around the fact that your kid is not being disabled to piss you off. He is how he is, and it is not a personal vendetta against you. Remember that changes in the plan are not always negative; some things can turn out better than you hoped.

For example, as I explained earlier, we moved to NYC to get my autistic son into a great school that we thought would help him. You can resent the fact that you had to move. Sure we gave up owning an actual brick house to live in a tiny pest infested apartment. But living here in NYC, we get to experience things I never imagined. I get to perform at actual comedy clubs, several nights a week. My daughter has joined the Museum of Moving Image. She has been to the MET numerous times and seen a dozen Broadway shows. We have done countless fun things because we live here. We moved here because we were trying to find better care for my son. Our "sacrifice" led us to some great things like living in NYC, a place where people come to vacation.

Things have changed. Many things for the worse; a few for the better. But almost everything will be different.

And always remember: this too will pass.

Your kid will get better, or you will get used to it. Or the Zombie Apocalypse will happen.

Either way, smile. Be content. Try to find joy like that of a child. Nothing lasts forever.

IMPROVE

I'm sure you've noticed by now that I have learned so much about how my son must see the world at home by going out and seeing the world for myself. Traveling is like watching TV on a moving couch, and my trip to China proved that. The country is so different it's almost surreal. I had to go to China because I had questions that needed answering. When stuff breaks in China do Chinese people say, "This piece of crap. All this stuff is made…here. By me." The answer is no. Also how do Chinese people fly like in the Crouching Tiger Hidden Dragon? And after a noon lunch are all Chinese people immediately hungry again at 1:30? How do you say "China" in Chinese? [vi]You know, real intellectual stuff.

Here are my thoughts as a simple man, with limited experience in China trying to sum up an 8000-year-old culture, in a few pages. Take these comments with a grain of salt.

Day One

Beijing airport is incredible. Granted, I flew out of the dump called LaGuardia. How an airport serving the largest city in the US can be worse than Love Field in Dallas, let alone a Guayaquil airport, or Beijing is beyond me. Charge an extra 20 bucks a ticket and make it so LGA does not look like you are going to get Hep B if you touch anything.

Sat next to a guy who works for FIFA (Fédération Internationale de Football Association). His job is to go to games and make sure everything goes well. Poor guy. Tough gig. Not sure I could handle just watching sporting events and traveling to exotic foreign countries, but I guess you get used to it. I am surprised he didn't burst out laughing when he tried to describe his job. What I understood is, basically, he watches the game. He doesn't run, doesn't ref, and doesn't even sell peanuts. Just watches. Cushy gig.

The flight was half full of Chinese kids. Not sure what they had been doing in the states. None of them spoke English. Smart kids, though.

All of them spoke Chinese; even the little ones. Here, I can't say two words in Chinese, and this little kid was spouting off like he was in the House of Flying Daggers. I really could have used subtitles (and some Red Vines).

There was one young Chinese girl on the flight who I believe was on the autism spectrum. She had many of the little telltale signs that autistic kids have, no eye contact, flapping of arms, and high pitch squeals. Her parents were having a difficult time controlling her. I sympathized with them. Pain unites us all.

After we landed two little Chinese men who spoke very little English picked me up from the Beijing airport.

On the way to the car I walked right by a man who picked up his son (he was maybe three years old) so the boy could pee…in a garbage can. The man caught my eye and smiled and I smiled back. Not sure what we were smiling about. Maybe that being a garbage collector in China is worse than in the US.

Day Two

I was up at 5 in the morning. Jet lagged.

For breakfast, I had this traditional Chinese dish that is a little like French toast.

That afternoon, I ate grilled scorpions and grasshoppers covered in hot sauce. The scorpions did not taste like much of anything. The grasshoppers tasted good. The consistency was firm but not too chewy, and the hot sauce gave it a nice kick. I'm not saying that I'm ready for the John the Baptist diet of only grasshoppers, but I knew I was going to try it again before I left.

I ate the grasshoppers with a friend of mine from college, Bruce Yee. It was good to catch up. Bruce is a Chinese American. We went to the market. I turned for just a second and lost him in a sea of 5'10" guys with short black hair.

"Bruce Yee!"

Nothing.

"Bruce Yee!"

A few heads turn, but none of them belong to Bruce.

"Bruce Yee!"

He waves from about 15 feet away. Thank goodness. I didn't want to yell Bruce Yee any more than I had to.

It sounded super racist to be in China and yell "Bruce Yee", which sounded an awful lot like a pasty white guy intentionally mispronouncing "Bruce Lee".

It's not cool to go to a market and start yelling the name of the most famous dead Chinese man of his generation. "Bruce Lee! Bruce Lee, where you at? Don't leave me hanging! Bruce, it's your boy Captain Kirk, where you at? Let's go shirtless and beat up eight guys, then go flying through the bamboo forest, or whatever you do here."

Not cool. Funny…but not cool.

For dinner, I ate at KFC. I know, I know. But in my defense, at dinnertime I was lost in a city with few signs in English, and fewer English speakers. I saw the KFC picture, needed to sit down and use the restroom, so I ate there too. Ok, there is no excuse. I checked for KFC's grasshopper poppers but couldn't find any.

Day Three

That was a rough day. I was on my feet for 14 hours. My calluses' calluses were getting calluses. That definitely did not help my boxing, but at least I could power walk to the ring. Nothing says "Scary Warrior" quite like power walking.

I walked by the Apple store in Beijing where there was a riot a few weeks before. I remember thinking at the time, "Why would people riot in China for the original iPhone when they could get a knock off for hundreds less?" Well now I know why. There is fake everything there; from fake Burberry to fake Beef, phony Prada to faux pork. But the one that really surprised me were the fake eggs. Yes eggs.

I asked my friend Bruce how much less could you make eggs for when the real ones only cost 10 cents each, to which he said, "Less." Ok, point taken.

When you cannot be sure whether or not your eggs are not some sort of Frankenstein-ian concoction made of chemicals, I understood being willing to pay for quality. I'm not saying we should all buy Apple stock, but many Chinese are convinced of the value of brand. I asked a sales person selling fake iPhones if she used one; she said, "No" and proceeded to pull a real one out of her purse. At more than a month's salary, I asked, "Isn't it expensive?" She said, "Yes." So I asked her, "Why buy the real one?" and without blinking she said, "It's better." Ok, there you have it.

Another thing that really stuck with me were the signs I saw in China. They had been literally translated into English losing their original meaning.

A very visible one in the park said, "No Naked Flamer".

The best I can figure out, they were trying to say:

Naked = Fine

Flamer = Fine

Naked + Flamer = Not Cool

Day Four

I had reserved the fourth day to check something big off my bucket list: a trip to a one of the wonders of the accident world, the Great Wall of China.

The Wall is truly an engineering marvel. It is obviously very long, and there are several places, coming from Beijing, where you can go see it. I saw it at Mutianyu. From the base, you can ride a ski lift to get to the top, and after looking around you, can ride down on a ski toboggan. A ride at the Great Wall? I know it sounds weird but it was tons of fun. I really let it fly on the way down. Probably not the best idea. Safety does not seem to be a big priority here. Maybe that's what happens when you have a country with a population numbering in the billions, where 100,000 people is a rounding error.

At the bottom, there were two guys dressed up in ancient warrior suits with fake swords coming to attack you. It was like the history channel meets Disneyland, weird but cool. The "ancient" warriors looked tough, and were even missing most of their teeth for added authenticity.

It was 14° F and very windy, factoring the wind chill, brought it down close to 0° F. As I was walking on the wall, I was asked by a group of Spanish guys to take their picture. One was taking off his shirt as I was walking up, but I never thought they would go for the Full Monty. They did. They got completely naked and then ran around like Mongolian invaders, yelling and spreading their bum cheeks. It made me miss my son, but I'm sure they all got pneumonia. After I took the picture, I started to run away like I was stealing their camera and they started to panic. One of the guys tried to run after me with his pants around his ankles. The others being naked, were not sure if they should give chase or put on their undies. It was funny. After the one giving chase fell down, I came back and gave them the camera. We are now Facebook friends.

I pictured them riding down on the toboggan, naked, like a Spanish version of Cool Runnings. I am sure the "ancient" warriors would flee before this unprecedented attack. If only the Mongolians had thought of that.

Day Five

What is on today's Chinese menu? The Forbidden City. Which is a bit of a misnomer. It is neither forbidden, nor a city. It was 25°F there, and no, there were no Spanish tourists requesting pictures be taken of their "Forbidden City." I did, however, see what looked like the Chinese version of the MTV show *Jackass*. It was a group of Chinese youth climbing on the marble structures and taking pictures. One of the youths was standing in front of a stone dragon pretending to make love to it.

I was a little surprised by their behavior because in general the Chinese people seemed very subdued, respectful and brainy. I mean, everyone speaks Chinese, and it is a hard language. (I thought about trying to learn it. The whole five-part Rosetta Stone is six bucks here.) I guess all over the world people are just people. Some smart people, some ding dongs. Apparently we don't have exclusive rights to being white trash.

That day's best "Chinglish" sign was on a menu: "Stir Fried Rape." I passed, just wasn't in the mood.

That was my last day there. It was time to go home. The trip was loads of fun, even if it was too short.

I did find out what Chinese people call their country. "China" is called "Zhong Guo" (which is something like middle country). I love how as Americans, we just change everyone's name.

US: "You say your name is 'Zhong Guo'? Not any more. Now it's 'China'. I don't care that it doesn't sound anything like 'Zhong Guo'.

We already changed it. Kindly write it on everything you make, like a junior higher would on his underwear when he goes to summer camp."

Countries name themselves in their own language. We named our own county and we did it in English obviously. This is the United States of America (or Estados Unidos de America, for those of you who have to press number two on your phone). At least "Estados Unidos" is a translation of "United States". With "China", it is not a translation, and it does not even sound like the former name. We just changed it.

That is what we do. We give other countries their English name (just like you do to your Indian friend at work). Sometimes, the change is reasonable. We asked France what their name was, and they said, "France" in French accent, and we said, no it's "France", in an English accent. But sometimes we just change it.

For example we asked the people from Finland what they called their country:
Finland: Suomi.
USA: I'm sorry, I didn't catch that. What do you call your country?
Finland: Suomi.
USA: Nope. Your name is Finland.
Finland: But we--
USA: Ahh ahk ahk, it's Finland. End of discussion.
Finland: But since the beginning we've been--
USA: (fingers in our ears) La, la, la. I am not listening. Oh sorry I did not see you there, FINLAND. You may go.
Ok, who's next? What's your country's name? Bundes Republik Deutschland?...(in high pitched voice) Nope, its Germany.
And how about you guys, Nippon Koku? Not anymore. Say hello to your new name...Japan. You just look Japanese.

How upset would you be if you went to Finland, being from America, and they said:
Finland: Where are you from?
USA: America.
Finland: You mean Obese-a-stan?

USA: What? No, America.

Finland: Oh, you mean Fatland; land of the lard, home of the fried.

USA: No, USA.

Finland: You mean Fatty, Fatty, Bubalaty, land of the dimpled buns?

As Americans we have a somewhat well deserved reputation abroad for being arrogant. Despite our reputation and the reception that accompanies it, I love to travel. And I can't help but feel that experiencing a culture that I don't completely understand gives me some level of insight into how our world must appear to my son.

I wonder though, if I love traveling so much, why do I detest being on airplanes? I have some unquenchable wanderlust that brutal air travel can't seem to destroy. It is the confinement to your seat that is required on an airplane that I hate; being forced to remain in one place. It is like you are a small child. It does not feel like prison, but more like afterschool detention. "Sit in your seat and think about what you just did. There will be no congregating around the bathrooms. Just sit there. Don't do this. Don't do that." Guessing it's a little like my son feels in school, all the rules without understanding what is behind them.

Why do I always fly the same airline? It is terrible. Am I a glutton for punishment? Or is it a case of the devil you know? Surely not all other carriers are this bad. Or are they? In a few weeks, I will be on a transatlantic flight to Istanbul on one of its competitors. I'm seriously considering taking a Xanax and trying to sleep the whole way. Why is flying difficult? The air is conditioned. There is food and drink. I have magazine and movies. Am I just conditioned to complain? Why do I feel so tired after doing nothing? Is the exhausting experience in my seat nothing more than the requirement to arrive at a new location?

I live an incredible life. Yet like everyone else, I have some struggles. Is it truly the struggles that make it great? Are we really little lumps of coal that need pressure and heat to produce the diamond that lies within? Is it possible to make a diamond without the crushing heat it normally requires? Why are we hard wired to avoid the pain that will inevitably produce the best version of ourselves? How come we constantly feel like the pressure will crush us? Is it possible for the pressure to crush us without producing that diamond? Does all struggle produce greatness? Or is it possible to struggle without any reward? If that is not possible, why do we not embrace the struggle? Why do we run from it instead of toward it? Is it possible that we spend our lives running from what would make us great? Is it possible that we don't know what we want or need?

I really needed to get off that plane.

For a while, despite my love of travel, I did not go anywhere. Some sort of masochism drove me to stay at home.

My self-flagellation played out as restricting the number of miles I ventured from my home. Somehow, my life's setbacks seemed to undermine my pursuit of the things I enjoyed. If I could give the Kirk from back then some advice about this, it would be the following:

Your life is not over. It is just beginning.

At first it does seem like your life is over (and life as you knew it - is).

It's bad. Trust me, I know.

When your autistic kid is 14, you still won't be able to leave him home by himself.

You'll still be wiping his bum when he is 12.

Your son never tells you he loves you.

Boo-hoo. I get it. Be sad for a while if you want, but eventually you have to get over it.

Life, like sports, is about adjustments. It's half time. You have to adjust.

Search, search, search for a babysitter. Try to guilt your family into doing it. Try to find a church with a monthly special needs childcare night.

Buy diaper wipes by the boxful to never be without them.

Hug your child (even against his will) when you want him to say I love you.

Yeah, that's bad, but it is not that bad. And things could be worse.

Don't agree?

What if you were the parent of an autistic kid…

who was also blind…

and you couldn't use your legs…

and you lived in the Congo…

during the war…

of 1665?

Yeah, I could go on. Clearly that is worse. No diaper wipes, no music videos, no medicine. Sure, no one cares that your kid is always naked, but your life expectancy is 30, and you never get to watch *Breaking Bad*. Oh the agony.

The saying is, "I cried because I had no shoes, until I met a man who had no feet."

My mom told me this expression when I was a kid and I used to always think, "Yeah, the guy has no feet now, but he probably started out with no shoes, stepped on a nail, got tetanus, and they had to amputate his feet." My mom said that is not what the saying means.

I think she is right.

There are people out there who are way worse off than you. Remember that. There is nothing special about you that protects you from being in their shoes (or lack thereof). That could be you.

Think you're a good person and that bad stuff can't happen to good people? Look up what happened to Job. No, not Steve Jobs. Job from the Bible (also in the Torah and Koran), a blameless (righteous, faultless, guiltless, unblemished) man. Blameless, and put through much worse than what you're going through.

Your life's not over. Make your halftime adjustments and keep moving.

Live life. You're not dead.

It's been said, "It is better to be a live dog than a dead lion."

The list of dead lions is long and impressive. The list of lions that death has recently claimed is celebrated:

Steve Jobs

Dick Clark

Whiney Houston

Who would have thought that Bobby Brown would out live Whitney Houston? This is a crazy world. (Say that out loud, "Bobby Brown outlived Whitney Houston." Weird, right?)

Yes, things have not turned out as planned.

Yes, you are not yet a lion. But you are still alive. You still have time. Things are still possible. Your final chapter has not yet been written.

My daughter is 15 and not yet an adult. I have tried to explain to her that she is not yet finished. She is not yet complete. Her clumsiness will go away. She will be less shy. She will find her calling. In short, she will grow.

That is also true for you and for me.

I am not yet done.

I am a work in progress.

I am trying.

I am moving.

Everyone is constantly in motion. You are either improving or deteriorating.

You either get better or you get worse. You never stay the same.

Improve. Grow. Stretch your wings. Be patient, and give yourself the space to grow.

No one knows what is around the corner.

This Dog's Life could still be turned into a Lion's Tale.

FOCUS ON THE POSSIBLE

There is a rumor that there is going to be a third Sherlock Holmes movie. We all know what the answer is going to be when producers ask a studio head, "Can we make another movie that mints money?" I enjoy the movies, but the BBC version with Martin Freeman and Benedict Cumberbatch (great name) is amazing, I highly recommend it.

While Cumberbatch is new to most of us, you have seen Freeman in the British version of *The Office*, and movies like *Love Actually* and *The Hitchhikers Guide to the Galaxy* among other things.

In this version the Sherlock Holmes character is either autistic or has Asperger's. He is almost completely lacking in empathy. While seeing every physical detail of his surroundings, he fails to see the emotions and feelings of a woman he works with.

She reaches out to him again and again and he just doesn't see it: he only sees the facts.

He has skills and abilities but some glaring weaknesses. He can see everything and nothing.

He can analyze every situation but the feelings of his own heart and soul.

Through deduction he can see the movements of others that have happened in other spaces and times, but he cannot see the effect his current coldness has on those closest to him.

He can see 10 steps ahead of his opponent but fails to see the breaking of a friend's heart occurring in his presence.

He has his strengths and his weaknesses.

It is the same with my son. We know his weakness, which are apparent to anyone who meets him. It's his strengths we are trying to find or develop.

We all, to some degree, can identify. Some of us are better at hiding our weakness than others, but like little blemishes in the armor of our personhood, they are there if you look closely. That is probably most people's greatest fear, getting close enough to another person that our flaws are obvious for all to see.

Having a handicapped child exposes even more of your flaws to the world.

When I am out with him in public it becomes clear that I, like everyone else, don't know what I am doing.

Listen, I don't know much. Even in the fields where my knowledge is strongest, I actually know very little.

Raising kids is not something I profess to know a lot about. Raising a severely autistic boy is something about which I know even less.

It is forcing me to come to grips with my flaws, and while not focusing on them, understand that they are part of what makes me human.

Sometimes I think that I try to avoid the trappings of an "autistic family", like that could somehow change my son's condition.

For example, I resent still having to buy baby wipes. My son was potty trained at age 12, when most kids are learning about fractions. But even now, we still have accidents. I am a bit of a germaphobe and don't even like wiping my own bottom, let alone someone else's. The baby wipes represent a very clear and present reminder that my life is not normal or regular. No matter what I tell myself, I am wiping another human's bottom with a wet wipe. But the thing is, when he does have an accident the wet wipes are a Godsend. Without them…well, I won't even go into the other options. So really I am only punishing myself. Whether or not

I get the wipes, my son is going to have accidents. I can get the wipes and move on, or I can choose not to get wipes and pretend that by not purchasing them it will somehow cosmically change the condition of my son's mind.

This goes back to the Serenity prayer. This is something I can control. I get the stupid wipes. If my son is miraculously healed from autism and I have a box of 10,000 baby wipes, I can give them away. Or better yet, hold a celebratory wipe-burning-bonfire, where we all dance around the fire naked like it's the *Lord of the Flies*, only with more pork and less death. (I always imagined the deaths in *Lord of the Flies* to have a kind of South Park "you killed Kenny" feel to them, where sure they were killed, but they would be back with no memories of their demise).

As usual, I am misdirecting my anger. The baby wipes are not the reason I wipe an extra bottom, any more than the label of "Autism" on my son, is not the reason he is autistic.

Younger Kirk, don't focus on what you can't control. Instead, only focus on what you can.

I am off to buy baby wipes in the city.

LOOK FOR ALLIES

In 1994 I traveled to Sri Lanka for the first time to meet my future wife's family.

People talk of the heat in Sri Lanka, but honestly I think Guayaquil is hotter. The smells and lack of personal space, however, was not something I was prepared for. Having grown up in a third world country, I thought all third world countries, everywhere were the same. I was wrong. So wrong.

Personal space is not something held in high regard in much of Asia. In Sri Lanka people think nothing of bumping into you. And they like to stare at you; not in a menacing way, but with interest. It's like they're trying to see inside you, past your transparent skin, to what makes the "Suda" ("Whitey") tick.

In Sri Lanka, telling the truth, no matter how harsh, is not considered insulting. Having not seen you in years, your friend might greet you with, "My, you are getting nice and chubby," and smile. Smile, not maliciously knowing that might hurt you, but smile because, well, you *are* getting nice and chubby, and now we all know it.

The brutal honesty was fine; what I had a hard time dealing with was the staring and people bumping into you in the street.

I went to seven grade schools and three high schools. I was always the new guy. Given my build, friendly attitude, and lack of backup, I was an easy target. I learned that I was not a good fighter, but that a butt kicking was not the end of the world.

The build up was always worse than the actual event. The event was over in a flash. Adrenaline simultaneously speeds things up and slows things down, turning a 2-minute fight into both a grueling ordeal and a flash in the pan--an accent for your day, nothing more. It's the reason your shirt is ripped and your nose is crooked, but not much more than that.

It is hard to come home and tell your dad, the pastor, that you, his son, have been fighting at school... again. It can't always be someone else's fault can it? Maybe I am starting these fights by having such a punchable face.

But I did learn a few things by being picked on. I learned how I preferred to lose a fight.

First of all, let's get this over with. Don't drag it out. The build up to the butt kicking is excruciating. You want to hurt me, fine. Just get to it. Don't tell me about it; show me. When? Why wait for after school? Now is good for me. Let's get this over so I can move on with my life. I live here now (at least until my parents decide I don't anymore), and I have other stuff to do.

Secondly, I learned most people, like me, despite what they say, don't like to fight. Sure they tell you they do. They "this" or they "that", but when it comes down to it, they like to *hit*, not *be hit*. Mostly, they don't like to be punched directly in the face. They like to win, but they don't necessary like the pain that comes with it. So if I am going to lose a fight (and I often did), I am going to make sure I try to punch the other person directly in the face, until I can't.

That is what grade school taught me as a weak foreigner.

Anyway, I did not realize it at the time, but this had made me a little sensitive. Testy, if you will.

If I interpreted someone's actions as threatening, I would go back to Rule One: Let's not drag this out. "If that is what you want, let's do it. No need to stand around and talk about it."

Let's get it all out and move on.

Well, actions that I would have interpreted as threatening during a particularly rough pick up basketball game in a poor part of town in the Americas were not meant that way in Sri Lanka.

For example, in Sri Lanka, that guy staring at me for the last 30 minutes is not "mad-dogging" me; he just does not see many people this shade of pink and wants to get a good look.

Those last three guys who have bumped into you are not trying to start something. There is just no place to walk and no concept of space.

That guys reaching into your pocket is not trying to rob....oh wait, no, he is...he is trying to rob you. Don't be stupid.

There were other differences between our families besides my wife's father's Sri Lankan culture. Her family led a very different life.

Her parents started an orphanage in the jungles of Sri Lanka in the 60s. And when I say "jungles", I mean jungles; with monkeys and cobras, out in the sticks. Where they were, there was no electricity for the first five years, no running water for the first six, and no cable...ever. In Guayaquil, I missed much of American culture, but forget about American culture; my wife missed *everyone's* culture. She even missed the corny sayings that even a square like me knew.

I had to explain there was a difference between what I would say, "You know what I mean, jellybean?" and her response, "I know what you are saying, jellybean." (Rhyme being the difference.)

Among other things, I remember having to explain a crude joke I made to her later.

Her: "Why did everyone laugh when you talked about sea anemones?"

Me: "What?"

Her: "Earlier, in the cafeteria, where people were laughing. You where talking about anemones."

Me: "Oh, not 'anemones', 'enemas'. Totally different."

Her: "How so?"

Me: "Well for one, Freud never recommended seafood."

Nothing. Blank stare.

So, yeah… She grew up in a jungle.

My wife remembers when her mother took in the first six orphan babies. There was no running water and all the babies were in cloth diapers. Her Swedish mom stood out front, stirring a cauldron with cloth diapers to disinfect them. The locals thought this white woman was crazy and would not last.

There was a war and many orphans. In short, the reason for this war was that the locals, in what was then called "Ceylon", would not work the tea estates, so the British brought in the Tamils from India.

When the English left, they left the Tamils in Sri Lanka. Injustice and discrimination turned to riots, and riots turned to war, turning a place once called "the Pearl of the East" into a place where teachers make $120 a month. A city considered by many to be far "ahead" of Singapore financially, was passed by that great Asian city a few decades later.

That is what war does. By definition, it destroys.

There was the Janathā Vimukthi Peramuṇa (thankfully called the JVP) insurrection, followed by civil war in the 80s. (There are better books than this describing the conflict. At least check the Wikipedia pages).

Basically, there was a race war between brown people and slightly browner people. To the untrained western eye there is no difference, but familiarity breeds contempt. We whites are not immune to it. No one hated the English more than the Irish or Scottish during their wars, and who could tell them apart? This reminds me of a joke from an early Simpson episode. Scottish groundskeeper Willie explains, "Brothers and sisters are natural enemies. Like Englishman and Scots. Or Welshman and Scots. Or Japanese and Scots. Or Scots and other Scots. Da** Scots! They ruined Scotland!"

Ask a Swede if he is German and he will make a face like he just ate pickled herring for the first time. They look alike, they both make good cars, but Swedes do not want to be Germans. In fact, Swedes don't even want to be Norwegians (like anyone more than 200 miles from the Arctic circle can even tell the difference).

So, this Swedish lady (who was either a saint or crazy, I can't decide which) started an orphanage out in the jungle, because, well, someone approached her with an orphan and she could not say no.

Someone donated the money for the first building and they just started taking in kids. At one point, there were over 50 kids in one three-bedroom house.

I always imagine it was like the old fairy tale: the old woman and the shoe, with so many kids she did not know what to do. Kids everywhere.

My wife grew up with people everywhere, sharing everything. Ownership was not a strict concept; rather more of an obscure guideline. For example, my wife talks about not having her own shampoo. It was her shampoo until someone else needed it; then it was their shampoo.

When it was time for someone to attend an event like a school graduation, everyone pooled his or her resources, including clothing.

I imagine it like Cinderella getting ready for that first ball, only with fewer birds and more monkeys.

Her parents had an old Range Rover that was broken down for weeks at a time, meaning they could not even go into the village. I'm telling you, this place was out there. It was the Jungle (with a capital "J").

To be honest, it sounds like my wife grew up on a crazy commune and I would condemn it if my mother-in-law was not one of the saintliest people I have ever met.

I remember one of the first times my wife's dad came to visit us after we had our second child. As he was leaving, I saw he had a nice blue hard side Samsonite suitcase like one I had.

Me: "Oh, wow, I have a suitcase just like that one."

He laughed, "Yes, yes, you do" and left.

It was not 'till later I realized I *had* a suitcase just like that one. One, which was now in Sri Lanka.

We had more than a few arguments about things he took.

"I think your dad stole my suitcase."

"What do you mean stole?"

"I mean, he stole it. As in, 'he took something that didn't belong to him.'"

"Oh, you mean he borrowed it?"

"Uhh, no I mean like "borrowed" without asking, with no intention of giving back."

"He might give it back."

"What? I think you are missing the point. He performed the Webster's definition of "stealing". Even if later he decides to give it back, it is still stealing."

"No, he can't steal from us. We are family"

Oh, boy. This was going nowhere.

"Ok, if you find out your dad is going to borrow anything else from me without asking, and never plans on returning it, could you please let me know?"

"Sure, no problem. Oh, I think he borrowed that briefcase you like. And your Leatherman tool. Yeah, I helped him pack that. There, I told you. Don't you feel better?"

For better or worse, my in-laws' hippy mentality has made me less materialistic.

I could not decide if that man was a thief or a saint, lifting things from my house that I was sure I needed, but in reality I never really missed. Hard to believe, but we can continue to live without a great deal of the things that we consider indispensible.

The civil war in Sri Lanka lasted for more than 30 years (much longer if you consider the conflict with the communists on the island before the race war). The war caused a diaspora of my father-in-law's people. He now has family living in Australia, New Zealand, America, Sweden, and particularly England.

His family in England has been there now for three generations. Some of the youngest generation seems about as Sri Lankan as I do, but with the oldest generation, old traditions diehard.

While living in Romania, we found out we were pregnant with our first child. Medical care in Bucharest at the time was disastrous. The hospitals were decimated, with basic things like clean sheets being over looked.

Call us crazy, but we decided to go back to America, get jobs and insurance, and have the baby on clean sheets.

On the way home from Romania, we stopped in London so I could meet some more of my in-laws. Most of them lived in South London, Tooting, to be exact. [hee, hee...tooting...]

It's one of those places that you know you need to be on your toes. Despite all the British politeness, there is a certain feel that people who have traveled off the beaten track recognize. Why are five grown men hanging out on a street corner at noon? Why is the music so loud? Oh yeah, because you're about to be robbed. It's that kind of place.

My wife's aunt, whom we stayed with, is a sweet lady who lives in her own little world which, to be honest, seems a lot more interesting than the one I live in. Sitting around with her adult children and some others, we watched a show with a little word play. Something funny was said, we laughed and she jumped in, "Why are we laughing? Because he is wearing a wig? Yes, Yes." No, not the wig, there was no wig. Not that we told her, though. We said, "Yes, the wig. Now keep watching."

From her house we went to a "party", and I say "party" in the loosest sense of the word. No dancing, no balloons, no cake, but there was food. And a lot of yelling, so I guess technically you could call it a "party".

It was the weirdest party I had ever been to, and I have been to some crackers.

Not a drop of alcohol but everyone was screaming. Just screaming. Talking, talking, talking. Everyone was talking to everyone and no one. People were just running their mouths but no one was listening. That was the weirdest part; no one was mad, they were just talking super loud and no one was listening.

The fact that the person they were talking to walked away or stopped listening was irrelevant. The fact that no one was listening would stop no one from talking. If someone at a party is screaming and no one is listening, does it make a sound? Yes, indeed it does. In fact, it is quite a cacophony.

Lady 1: Have you seen Shandrica's baby, so fair and chubby.

Lady 2: I think (pronounced tink) this chicken curry has too much salt.

Lady 1: It is like a little ball of cheeks and love, precious child.

Lady 3: Weather was nice, today, not too cold. I don't like it when it's too cold. What is it like now? (moving her head to look out the window)?

Lady 2: I think it was brought by Jason's wife. This one (pointing at Jason's wife). She has never known how to cook.

Lady 3: My goodness, look how dark it is outside.

The food was excellent, even the salty chicken curry. There was every kind of curry you can imagine, but if you don't like curry you're out of luck, because that was all there was.

One of my wife's long lost relatives, who said she was 80, but looked like she might have gone on a double date with Methuselah, gave us 20 pounds. I am not saying she was old but she was Moses's babysitter. Zing (sorry, couldn't help myself).

So 20 pounds, all the curry you can eat, and I got to watch multiple blue hairs have three different conversations, by simultaneous screaming? Winner winner, chicken dinner, it was a good party.

If I could give some advice to a younger me it would be: try not to judge. When you judge you tend to view everyone through the prism of your experience. It is hard to avoid. You have had experiences that are real and honest but not everyone has had those experiences. Their experiences may have led them down a different path. They may have arrived at the same place as you but from a different direction.

Not everyone eyeballing you is looking for a fight. Not everyone bumping into you is trying to put you in your place. They may just be walking on this crowded little path that is life where fate has forced them to rub elbows with you. Keep an open heart and mind, you may find someone to fight alongside of you, not against you.

DON'T WORRY

Working at the orphanage in Romania seems like a million years ago. These days I work for a school. When I am not wrestling with my son or trying to help my daughter with math homework I don't understand, I work for a school in Ecuador.

Previously, I had that corporate job (the one that moved me to the UK remember?), for around a decade. They moved me around quite a bit and we ended up in the Big D (no, not Dysentery; Dallas).

It was good for what it was, but it was unfulfilling. I was ready for something different.

I was looking for a job that was not mind numbing; and something where I did not feel like a little bit of my soul died everyday, or at least did not make me feel like I wanted to kill myself every Monday morning.

I am not an expert, but it does not feel healthy to sit in your car in the parking lot before going into work on Mondays, yelling and hitting the steering wheel with your head. That is normal right? Everyone does that before they go into the office, right?

I started thinking about what I wanted to do and felt I would like to give something back. I spoke with my Dad who is still working in Ecuador, running a school and a church. It is a school that in the afternoon serves underprivileged kids on scholarships, giving them a chance at life through education. He was looking to expand the school. He asked if I would be interested in helping with the fundraising.

It is hard to describe, but I felt a peace about it and decided to give it a shot.

So that is what I do during the days, when JJ is not at home, having a fit, needing his clothes changed or hands washed.

Several times a year, I will get together a team of people who want to go build a class room together, and that is what we do. We travel down, and for a week try to have a small impact by doing something positive for someone else in a concrete way. I serve as the guide, translator, driver, errand boy, etc.

You would be surprised at the variety of people who want to come down on these trips. You get the pious, the people searching, the twelve steppers, the people angry to be there, and everyone in-between.

We had a team from Odessa, Texas come down. They were a hoot. The team included a father and his two sons in their early 20s. I think he wanted them to come down in the hope that it would straighten them out. The older one loved his chewing tobacco, and the younger his ultimate fighting.

The older one was about 6' 2", thin but tough. He was always trying to hide his chewing tobacco habit from me, leading him to accidently swallow his chew once when I walked up on him unexpectedly. I played dumb and let him cough it out.

"You Ok? Everything alright?" I couldn't help but smile a bit.

"Yeah, yeah, I'm fine. Just a little bit of a cough."

Yeah? A cough induced by swallowing tobaccy? It wasn't that big of a deal. The goofier part was him swallowing tobacco juice to hide it. But if that made him feel better, I was not going to stop him.

Towards the end of the trip, I asked anyone if they were sick, so we could get parasite medicine for them in Ecuador where it was readily available. Tabaccy Joe raised his hand.

"Yeah, I'm little sick."

"How bad? Do you need to see a doctor? What kind of sick?"

"I'm the kind of sick you get when you drink 30 Coors Light."

I wanted to ask, what kind of sickness is that? Sounds like you're suffering from stupidity, for which there is no cure.

But what I really said was: "Uhh, ok. What kind of sick is that? Is it bad?"

"Yeah well, water's shooting out my butt. Could do with some Kaopectate (he pronounced it Kao-petid). Like to get down to what it's like when you drink 12 Coors."

And there you have it. A diagnosis of an illness based on how many alcoholic beverages you have consumed. I suppose Chemo patients feel like "they just drank a fifth of Jack" and bipolar sufferers are the "kind of sick where you dropped some bad acid."

But it was the younger brother who was the live one. He was 5' 7", about 130 pounds of wire and sinew. His face was accented by a red beard and matching Mohawk. He was 20 and a pro fighter in the east Texas MMA circuit. Something told me he was fighting mostly on raw wildness and energy more than technique. I'm guessing he had not studied at the feet of a wise Kung Fu master, but that didn't mean he couldn't "kick those Kung Fu students where the sun don't shine".

He was an ornery little fella. I nicknamed him "Deliverance", in homage to the movie of the same name. Not to his face, of course. I'm not an idiot. But in print, I'll call him "Deliverance." I'm guessing he is not going to be reading this. In fairness, nicknames for tough guys who are not Rhode Scholars are best hidden where they won't find them--in books.[vii]

The trip with these good old boys was fun.

There was a different guy on the team who insisted on making racist comments. After a while I did not know what to do with the comments, so I just stared at him blankly. You can only correct people on their racism a few times before you realize enlightenment is probably not in the cards. One of my conversations with him went about like this:

Me: "That pejorative is derogatory."

Simple man: "I know they's derogatory, that's why I vote Republican."

Churchill said that the best argument against democracy is a 5-minute conversation with the average voter. I would say that is the best argument against many things, including public schools, tobacco and Ed Hardy t-shirts.

A couple of them were confused on a few issues but they were good guys. Guys who came down on their vacation time and spent their own money to try to do something for someone else. They had their hearts in the right place, no matter how ignorant that one guy sounded at times. More polished people talk a good talk about giving or doing something, but don't always show up. At least these guys showed up. Actions speak louder than words.

Working on the site with them was a trip. We were pouring a concrete floor that was covered in rebar. There were steel rebar pieces sticking straight up about fourteen inches off the ground. It was late in the afternoon, we were all tired, splattered with concrete, trying to finish up. Out of the blue, Deliverance jumped up on his older brother's back administering a rear naked choke. Not a piggyback ride, but a full on, forearm-and-bicep-against-the-jugular submission maneuver.

Big brother had a metal tool in his hands at the time, a long piece of bent rebar used for lifting the rebar mesh off the ground as the cement is poured. He started to stumble as the little Tasmanian devil on his back tightened his grip; his boots slogging through newly poured concrete, face turning pink, and his tool flailing around wildly.

I was surprised. I don't mind a good fight. Shoot, my brothers and I used to fight all the time. Our favorite fighting game was called "Voltron". Basically my two younger brothers and their best friend Carlos would try to attack me and I would fight them off. *Voltron* was a Japanese cartoon that involved multiple robots who would join to fight as one. I know, thin, but we were kids; that is what we called it.

But this was no "Voltron". These were not kids. We were on a construction site with exposed rebar everywhere, sharp tools, and any number of ways to put an eye out.

As big brother pushed back against the wall trying to grind the little parasite off, I was sure they were going to fall on the exposed rebar, impaling both of them, and then I would have to try explain to the authorities how these two Gringos got impaled on the same iron rod.

"You see, Deliverance is an ultimate fighter and thought it would be funny to try to render his brother, who has a mouth full of tobacco, unconscious; and his brother didn't appreciate it, so he impaled both of them. Funny story, right?"

I called over to their dad who was standing a few feet from me, but also had a good view of the action.

Me: "You see what's going on?"

Texas father: "Yeah, I see it. "

Big brother Dave was starting to turn purple and his staggering had slowed.

Me: "Should we do something?"

Their father pondered my question for a brief second. "He knows he should tap out." And with that bit of knowledge, went back to his work. I stood there, frozen; sure I was watching a modern day reenactment of Cain and Abel.

Abel dropped to his knees and sure enough, he tapped out. Cain jumped off his back, chuckled a little, and went back to pouring concrete.

Abel's color came back and he stood back up.

Me: You alright?

Abel: Yeah, got c-ment everywhere. (Turning his attention to Cain) Look what you done. I got c-ment in my boots. C-ment on my socks too, you idiot.

He did. In addition to having almost died, he did, in fact, have "c-ment" in his boots and on his socks.

Abel: Sneaky little runt, sneaks up on me when I am not looking. Can't do that when I'm ready for ya.

Cain: Don't have to. You never pay attention.

Abel: Sneaky.

Cain: Put your little candy a** to sleep.

Abel: Did not.

Cain: Only 'cause you tapped.

Abel: Let's go again.

Cain: Let's do it.

At this point their Dad looked up, "This c-ment ain't going to pour itself....Boys, get to working."

And that was the end of that. Clearly this was not the first time this had happened.

Abel did tap.

They didn't die.

Apparently father still knows best.

Another time, we had a team of great guys from Louisiana who brought their own spices for all their meals. The brand was called "Dirt", and it was liberally applied to everything before they had even tried it.

We had another group that came down and was in disbelief that everyone didn't speak English.

Confused traveler: "You mean their English is not good?"

Me: "No, I mean it's nonexistent."

Confused traveler: "So you mean their grammar is incorrect and they have limited vocabulary?"

Me: "No. I mean they have no vocabulary, and their grammar is irrelevant because they have no vocabulary."

Still confused traveler: "Are you sure?"

Me: "Am I sure that the Spanish, not the English, came to South America and colonized it forcing everyone to learn their language? Yep, pretty sure."

I joke about the Deliverance boy and his brother but they impressed me. They did something. They got out of their comfort zone and did something. That is something I would tell my younger self to do.

Try. You don't know what you are capable of doing 'till you try. Move out of familiar territory and spread your wings. Don't pigeon hole yourself with what you have done in the past. Don't worry about what others say about you. You can't make everyone happy. If you ask those good old boys' friends if they would be a good fit for charity work they would probably laugh; but the jokes on them. Those boys worked (and played) hard. They gave something back, while being themselves. They didn't allow other people's judgments of them dictate how they lived their lives. Neither should you.

AIN'T OVER 'TILL IT'S OVER

Parenting, particularly parenting an autistic child, is hard. My son is no longer a boy; physically he is a man. He may have the mind of a boy, but he has the body of a man. He likes to wear adult pajama bottoms, the ones that have the little opening for going pee. He likes how the flannel material feels.

He has the tactile issues, common for kids with autism. As I best understand it, he can feel his clothes rubbing against his body at all times. A regular person does not feel their clothes on them at all times, at least not as intently. As I sit here writing this, I don't really feel my clothes unless I think about it. I know they are there, and perhaps more importantly I know when they are not there, but rough jeans don't bother me. Once they are on, they are on; I don't give it another thought. Not him. He can feel the jeans on him at all times.

It's different, but it's part of the journey we are on. It does, however, present problems from time to time.

He rides a little bus to school every morning at 7:30, and returns home around 3:30. He has an aide who has to ride with him, without the aide he would get naked.

I went to get him off the bus recently and the aide who rides the bus looked perplexed. She was not saying anything, but something was not right, and I could not figure out what until he got off the bus. He ran down the stairs of the bus and jumped off the last step. He landed, feet spread, groin first, pointing with both hands at the little opening the pj's have for going pee.

I could immediately see what he was pointing at. He had a full erection through the pjs' zipper area and he was proud of it. This was not a little boy erection; he is physically now a man and he wants to show the world. And he was smiling. Not in a creepy way, just happy. It's something new. He built this. "Look what I did!"

Me: "Ok, yes, I see. Put it away now."

But he thinks I cannot see it, or don't understand, so he points at it again, with both hands, thrusting his pelvis further forward.

The aide in the bus did not know where to look. Maybe she has never seen a man's penis before; but she has now, and she looks terrified.

Me: "Ok, we all see. Very nice. Now put it away. Good job, now put it away."

With that, he grabs his waistband, pulls it out, and immediately releases it, snapping it and everything else back into place, and walks off like he has been doing that all of his life. Like a boss.

What are they teaching him at this school? Are there Magic Mike stripper lessons?

The unusual clothing selections are not the only side effects of the tactile issues. He also wants constant positive stimulus input.

As best I understand it, autistic kids have a hard time getting stimulus from the outside world and knowing where their body ends (this is one of the reasons they bang their heads, to get input).

One of the things that helps with this tactile input is joint compression, or being hugged, squished, or sat on. The pressure helps them feel better (which is also the reason they like the water--it "hugs" them).

When he was little, he liked being tickled, which has basically turned into wrestling and can be a little physical. I remember the first time he gave me a shiner. Just under my right eye. It was a nice one. Worse than the ones I get boxing.

Wrestling is one of the weirdest side effects from autism. For him, it provides the stimulus input needed.

Some lady invented a hugging machine, which I thought was cool, until I thought, "or you could get a human to hug you for free."

Well he's really taken to the "wrestling", and now, everyday, he wants to wrestle, all the time. He wants to roll around on the ground shirtless, like we are Lucha Libre fighters on Univision.

But with his lack of speech it is like *Rain Man* meets Lucha Libre.

In this corner, hailing from Guayaquil, he enjoys playing *Sid Meier's Civilization*, basketball and doing the Macarena, Kirk "Tighty Whities" Smith.

And in this corner, he likes Hot Wheels cars, swimming naked, and You Tube videos, JJ "Nacho Libre" Smith.

Little known fact: "Nacho Libre" is Spanish for, "Chubby Thunder", which, I suppose, would make me "Esqueleto" ("Skeleton Man").

I often have cuts or black eyes. No, it's not because I don't know that "No" means no; its because my son likes to fight. I don't know where he gets it, but he is one of the reasons I try to stay in shape.

Not sure if my son's autism is related to my undiagnosed ADD, but boy it hits me hard sometimes.

The first five minutes of my day often look like this:

I open my computer to check my email.

What is this? A shipping status email from Amazon? Let's just check the status of that shipment.

What? There is another tab open to Yahoo sport? Why not check the scores real quick. Johnson's injured?

That reminds me, Thomas is injured. I should update my fantasy team. Uh-oh, new message in the league mailbox from Michael.

Oh that reminds me, Mike messaged me late last night and I didn't get back to him. Oh, Mike wants me to open for him next Monday. I should put that on the calendar. Ok, wrote it on the calendar.

What is that on the calendar, next week is my brother's birthday. I should really order something for him. Amazon is still open. Good. I wonder if there is something good on Woot. Travel headphone? Nah.

That reminds me, I'm in San Francisco next weekend and I didn't make the car reservation. Get on the airline website, so I get my points. There is a great sale on the homepage to Mongolia.

I have always wanted to go Mongolia. I wonder what it is like. Quick, check Lonely Planet. But where would I stay? I should check airbnb. What is my password? I think they emailed it to me. While I'm in my email I should…this goes on indefinitely.

My wife thinks I am faking it.

This was an actual conversation we had.

Her: Where are you going in the car? I thought you were going to do the dishes?

Me: I was going to do the dishes, but then I was thinking I should get some new sponges. I went outside to go to the car and saw my motorcycle. I have not started the bike in a while, so I started it. Then I realized I should replace the left mirror, but I need a special tool. I am going to the motorcycle shop.

Her: Fine, get some sponges next door and don't get them at Target or that will be the rest of your day.

Then I am off to the Bronx Target. Yes there is a Target in the Bronx. I know what your thinking about the Bronx, but don't be scared for me. I am fine. My wife, whose skin adsorbs much more light than mine (and contains more melanin), was concerned about safety when we moved here.

Not her safety, but my safety. She said, "Me and the kids will be fine, we blend. I am worried about your pink hiney. You're going to need a rape whistle."

In my defense, I have never needed a rape whistle. I am a very fast runner.

Running is great for the body and serves a purpose, but there are some things you can't escape by running.

In 2006, my wife went to the doctor for some routine tests. She had abdominal pain. The pain turned out to be annoying but harmless cysts on her ovaries. However, the ultrasound revealed a bigger problem. She had a tumor. Cancer was growing in her uterus.

We found out several years before that she had Endometriosis, hardening of the uterus walls. The issue with the cysts had brought to light the more serious problem requiring immediate surgery.

I was in complete denial. It was not possible. There is no way she can die and leave me a widower raising two kids, one of whom is severally handicapped. Trying to split the duties between the two of us is overwhelming. Apart, it would be impossible.

I just denied it. I didn't see it at the time, but in hindsight I just ignored it. It was not happening. She was not sick, and it was certainly not life threatening. It was one of my most shameful moments. I acted as if a real and present danger to my wife was not even there.

Surgery was successful at removing the tumor, but not my shameful behavior.

I often reflect on the mistakes I have made and my inability to "fix" areas of my life and I have come to the following conclusion: When trying to complete a task that is unachievable or outside of my capabilities, I remind myself, "It's not enough, but it's the best I can do." I often feel this way.

The pressure can be overwhelming. Especially the kind we put on ourselves.

When is enough, enough? I would put forward: Never.

There is never a time when all will be accomplished. It is not like anything can ever be accomplished that would bring an end to the chase.

Every Type A knows, finishing one goal only opens the door for the next. There is an endless list of things to check off.

You finished the blog? Turn it into a book.

Finished the book? Turn it into a movie.

Movie done? Time to run for office.

Presidency over? Time to bring peace to the Middle East and invent the next Snuggie.

I always focus on the accomplishment, the destination, the checkmark on the page. But the checkmark is nothing. The checkmark is boring.

How did you get to the check mark? What is the story? That is what intrigues me.

We are all on a different journey. Mine just happens to be a million miles from normal. Raising an autistic teenager is not your everyday journey.

However, it is just that: a journey. And it's an interesting journey. I try to remind myself to forget the checkmark and enjoy the ride.

Remember, it's hard to top the great Limey Drunk:

Success is not final, failure is not fatal: it is the courage to continue that counts.

Winston Churchill

My Thanks

Mom and Dad, thank you for everything, duh. But also, Mom, thank you for your help finding the difference between were, where, there and their.

Family extended and immediate thank you, there, done. Joking but seriously my family is my strength and I am not just talking about blood. As you get older you chose much of your "family" by spending time with them. Thank you for your encouragement and positivity.

Todd Schoenberger the cop with the heart of gold and the winning smile. Ok maybe not a heart of gold but great smile...since the braces. Your help turning this pile of words into something semi-coherent is greatly appreciated. I didn't realize how far I had to go until...you told me. Seriously, thank you.

To the many people who are helping me on this comedy journey. Linda Stogner from Backdoor, Randy Butler from Hyenas. JR and Richie Tienken for making me feel at home at the Comic Strip. It is my NYC comedy home, a place to get laughed at on and off stage, thank you.

Jason Leary, thank you for the editing help (but if you find typos blame him, Todd and my mom).

And finally, my wife. She is concerned that this book will read like I am somehow a single father doing it all on my own, poor me. Let me assure you, that is not the case, she does more than her share. I probably do 20% of the work around here; the fact that I find the 20% so overwhelming is an indictment of me, not her. She is concerned that the book does not paint a balanced picture. I wrote this book from the only point of view I could, mine. It is not fair or balanced but I hope it is funny. My wife will write a book too someday. Her book will be different. It will be a lot better, and have bigger words; it will be balanced, more heartfelt and prize winning, but not as funny. For a great rebuttal read hers.

That being said: wife, thank you. Thank you for pushing me to write, be honest, find my voice; encouraging me to finish and spending the advance (if only there was one). Feelings come in waves, rising and falling like the tide. We have been through good times and bad. There are few people who stand by your side and fewer who stand by you at low tide. I feel fortunate that such a beautiful, smart, articulate woman chose to stand by my side. (That has to be worth a month of household chores.)

And to the rest of you, you know who you are, who are (accidently) hilarious and are included in this book, thank you. Some names have been changed to protect the guilty and the innocent…me.

About the Author

Kirk Smith and his family live in the East Bronx, in a third story walk up, above his Albanian landlady. Some day he will write about the crazy things going on in the floors below him (after he moves to safety). He sometimes tells jokes, anecdotes and embarrassing stories all over the country. In NY City he can often be seen at the Comic Strip. He also likes to travel to South America to build stuff. In South America he can mostly be seen in Ecuador.

i Ralph Waldo Emerson
ii Autism Society of America 2012
iii Autism Society of America website 2012
iv I am indebted to Albert Camus's *The Myth of Sisyphus*. (Although I do not agree with everything in the book, chapter 4 is eye-opening.)

v God in the Dock: Essays on Theology and Ethics. By C. S. Lewis
vi I know I know Mandarin and Cantonese
vii if you (you know who you are and your real name), if you find this end note, I'll send you a case of these books ☺